The Dawkins Delusion Exposed

Richard Dawkins Unmasked -
His Faith, His Religion, His God, His Fanaticism
and the Hidden Agenda, Irrefutably Exposed at
Last; Once and for All.

Christopher Eckstein RT(R) ARRT

Caution:
Atheists that read this book will
likely become creationists.

PRESS

Chapter One

Chapter Two

Chapter Three

Chapter Four

Chapter Five

Chapter Eight
Evolutionism, The Most Hostile Religion

Chapter Nine
Government Mandated Religion

Chapter Ten
The Gap Delusion

Preface

I read Dawkins' books preparing my mind to be chal-
lenged by scientific evidence that may give one cause
to consider evolution. I was really surprised to learn that
such a huge religion was being spiritually nourished by
such simple rants and insults. Dawkins plugs a lot of 50
cent words into his fluff, granted, but is this really the best
case that evolutionism can make against creation? After
investigating three decades of Mr. Dawkins' work, I have
tied together a very sound and disturbing case against
this man, his religion and the culture that embraces his
fanaticism. This book is the key that unlocks the mystery
of modern evolutionism.

The foundation that evolutionism is built on does not
even exist. Why such an enormous cult following to this
baseless religion? The answers may surprise you, but
there are good reasons why 75% of youth who attend
secular college will denounce their faith in a Creator
within one year.

You know who Richard Dawkins is. You know what
he claims to believe. Now know that in 10 short chapters
everything that Richard Dawkins claims to believe about
science and religion is going to be turned inside out and
fully exposed.

Let us don our x-ray specs and look deep into the mind and soul of this religious guru that has spent decades masquerading as a scientist. Prepare to meet Dawkins unmasked. If it is your desire to pierce the cloak of deception and shine the light of truth on the most dark and dangerous religion that this planet has ever known, then all you need to do at this point is to start turning pages. Enjoy the ride. Buckle up, the road is going to get bumpy.

www.thedawkinsdelusionexposed.com

Chapter One

A Deeply Religious Delusion

Was Einstein an Atheist?

T he first words of chapter one in Richard Dawkins' book *The God Delusion* are a quote from the famous and accomplished physicist, Albert Einstein. Dawkins attempts to drag Einstein into the atheist camp even though Einstein never claimed to be an atheist. Dawkins was unable to tie evolutionism to any of Einstein's work. Let's take a look at the quote from Albert Einstein.

I don't try to imagine a personal God; it suffices to stand in awe at the structure of the world, insofar as it allows our inadequate senses to appreciate it. -Albert Einstein

This quote means that Einstein was an atheist? Is this Dawkins' best case for implying that Einstein was an atheist? Keep in mind a structure requires a designer or at least a con-struction worker, would it not? Its seems clear that Einstein did not envision a personal Savior, understood. Some people believe that God is some sort of Genie in a bottle, and my guess is that this was not Einstein's view of God either, however, Einstein did not reject all of the overwhelming scientific evidence of a Creator and pronounce himself an atheist. Dawkins tries to lead the reader to believe that Einstein was an atheist. My guess is that Dawkins is unaware of other statements made by Albert Einstein that point to the contrary.

People like us, who believe in physics, know that the distinction between past, present, and the future is only a stubbornly persistent illusion. - Albert Einstein

Albert Einstein seems to be very aware of a dimension or dimensions outside of our reality. This is strong evidence that Einstein would have favored the idea of a Creator, as opposed to naturalistic processes over billions of years. Einstein never promoted the doctrine of uniformitarianism. Einstein never said that the present is the key to understanding the past, he seems to hold the view that the past, present and future are indistinguishable. This view simply does not fit into the parameters of the evolutionism scheme. I have another quote from Albert Einstein.

Of all the laws of physics, the two laws of thermodynamics will never be negated or replaced. - Albert Einstein

Einstein fully understood the laws of thermodynamics. Einstein was fully aware that everything is winding down, cooling off, and burning out, with no matter or energy creating itself. The above quote is a clear declaration of this view. It would be inconceivable to reason that Einstein might have believed that the universe created itself. See chapter three's *Laws of Thermodynamics* for greater elaboration on the topic.

I noticed that "enlightened scientists" always quote Einstein in their work, and I just couldn't resist hopping on the Einstein band wagon. So, Einstein was possibly an atheist, and there you have it ladies and gentlemen, proof for evolution. Einstein never declared himself to be anti-creation. No amount of wishful thinking by Mr. Dawkins can change this fact. For fun, let us suppose that Einstein was a devotee to evolutionism. Would that prove that a living organism created itself from dirt some 4 billion years ago and met another living organism of the opposite sex, that happened to spring out of the dirt soup at the same time and have kids? Not only would these two organisms of the opposite sex have to spring out of the dirt soup at the same time, but being oxygen dependent, they must have had oxygen producing plants spring up at the same time to give them their much needed oxygen... But how could the plants have sprung up without the much needed carbon dioxide given off by breathing animals? Wow, this is all too much deep thinking for a superstitious person like myself. A symbiotic relationship coming into existence by pure cosmic magic. Plants cannot live without animals, animals cannot live without plants. It is just so obvious that it is not possible for this to get started without some kind of major intelligent direction. Why in the heck would any rational person call this impossibility science and teach it to the youth as if it were fact? How could anyone disagree with the fact that this scenario is pure religious faith? The grand delusion. I don't believe that a thinking man like Einstein ever swallowed it, or he would have said so. In this book, I will expose facts to reveal that Mr. Richard Dawkins himself does not even swallow it, he is merely selling it.

The Birth of a Religion

On the second page in chapter one of Dawkins' book *The God delusion* we find Dawkins quoting the greatest prophet of his chosen religion, you guessed it, Charles Darwin, the "racist", sexist. By the way, Charles Darwin did not have a degree in science, he had a degree in theology. I must commend Dawkins that he did make it to the second page of the first chapter before expressing his clear adoration for this great prophet of evolutionism. Dawkins references Charles Darwin's book *The Origin of Species*. Come on now Richard, tell us the original name of the book. Why was it chopped down to only four words by the sixth edition? Why? Because the real title strongly alludes to the true intent and ultimate goal of the evolutionism religion. The original title of the book by Darwin was *The Origin of Species by Means of Natural Selection or the Preservation of Favored Races in the Struggle for Life.* Preservation of favored races? What's that mean? That could probably be well defined by Adolph Hitler, Joseph Stalin or Pol Pot. They were all excited about the preservation of favored races. Make no mistake, evolutionism is a religion, a religion that seems to have a clear agenda. When empowered mad men that adhere to this ideology unleash their evolutionary schemes, millions and millions of innocent people die, you know, in order to preserve the "favored races". Is Dawkins really ignorant of these facts? Perhaps Dawkins is fully aware of these facts and deems himself of a favored "race". Perhaps Dawkins likes the idea of preserving favored humans and exterminating the ones that are not more like him. Mr. Dawkins chose to use the following quote from Charles Darwin's book: *The Origin of Species by Means of Natural Selection or the Preservation of Favored Races in the Struggle for Life;*

Thus, from the war of nature, from famine and death, the most exalted object which we are capable of conceiving, namely, the production of higher animals directly follows. There is grandeur in this view of life, with several powers, having been originally breathed into a few forms or into one; and that, whilst this planet has gone cycling on according to the fixed law of gravity, from so simple a beginning endless forms most beautiful and wonderful have been and are being evolved. -Charles Darwin

And there you have it ladies and gentlemen, the birth of a new religion. A religion that includes a plan for man's salvation. The death of other humans is the means to superiority. To be exalted to a higher animal, lots of other animals must die. How ridiculous is that? When and how has that ever been proven in science or in any capacity? It simply does not happen. After Nazi mad man Adolph Hitler murdered over six million Jews, did any homo sapiens sapiens emerge? (We're gonna keep adding sapiens because that implies that humans are evolving in intelligence). Nope, no super humans emerged. No nazis sprouted wings or had an increase in brain size. One could reason that the lower life forms were the ones doing the killing. Anyone that claims that evolutionism is science is clearly blinded by their faith in that religion, and oh how blinding misguided faith can be. I revere a God of life, light and love. This god of evolutionism is the god of death, darkness, and suffering.

One may engage debate by saying, *"Well many wars have been fought in the name of religion"*, and my response to that would be, yes I agree, and the religion of evolutionism is no exception. The fact is, the evolutionism religion has claimed more lives of the innocent than all the other wars throughout human history combined. Other religion's atrocities pale in comparison to the sheer insanity that has been unleashed upon humanity by the religion of evolutionism. Not driven just to gain land or treasure, but for the exaltation and preservation of the more highly evolved homo sapiens species. Evolution is moving us toward god status. If we just keep killing off the "inferiors", then surely we will one day be exalted to god status, you know, buzzing about the cosmos at warp speed like in Super Mario Galaxy, achieving immortality through our highly evolved longevity technology advancements. The ends certainly sounds like humanism at its core, granted, but the means? The means sounds so demonic no matter how you try to spin it. I can use a word like demonic because I make no effort to be politically correct or polite. Why should I try to be politically correct? Charles Darwin made no effort to be politically correct when he wrote these words...

"At some future period, not very distant as measured by centuries, the civilized races of man will almost certainly exterminate and replace the savage races throughout the world." Charles Darwin, *The Descent of Man*

This almost sounds like a declaration of war, or a proposal to start the extermination of the less evolved *"savage races"*. This seems to be the inspiration that a Nazi mad man needed to exact his plans to systematically exterminate the non Aryan population. I will not go out of my way to offend Mr. Dawkins, but nor shall I don kid gloves to confront the sheer insanity that has been inflicted upon humanity by the greatest mass murderers that this world has ever known, who were totally devoted to the religion of evolutionism.

"A direct line runs from Darwin, through the eugenics movement - Darwin's cousin, Francis Galton- to the extermination camps of Nazi Europe." Martin Brookes, *'Ripe Old Age' New Scientist*

Richard Dawkins was a guest on the on the O' Reilly Factor on April 23rd, 2007 and he actually tried to disown Hitler (its on youtube). Sorry Richard, Hitler is all yours. I'm surprised that Dawkins is unaware that Hitler was trying to produce a "race" of super humans by Darwinian methods. Is Dawkins clueless about history and Hitler's agenda, or is Dawkins lying? We know that Adolph Hitler wrote a book called *Mein Kampf*. Please understand that in German the words *mein kampf* mean *my struggle*. Interesting, and what was that struggle for? Ah yes, the struggle for the preservation of the *"favored races"*. Adolph lifted this idea and these words from the title of Charles Darwin's book, *The Origin of Species by means of natural selection or the Preservation of Favored Races in the **Struggle** for Life*. Charles Darwin is the key religious leader that I would credit for the birth of evolutionism. Hitler was a big Charles Darwin fan. Hitler's main intent was to create a master "race" of humans, producing *"higher animals"*, by means of exterminating the *"savage races"*. Hitler's religion was admittedly evolutionism. Isn't that sly, the way Mr. Dawkins tries so hard to disown Adolph Hitler (one of his own) and adopt Albert Einstein (who was probably theist)? How is Dawkins different than any other religious leader who lies and misleads people to win devotees to their ideology? I am not naive enough to believe that any of the world's religions are without these dishonest con men.

Dawkins is a product of the evolutionary seminary; the public schools and universities. Dawkins has been indoctrinated into his beliefs by an "education" system, as are many of the children receiving a public education, today more than ever. There is strong evidence that Dawkins has never done any deep thinking for himself, as he so often implies. I am sure that Dawkins aspires to be one of the great prophets of evolutionism like Darwin or Lyell. The problem for Dawkins is that he does not have any scientific discoveries or even a neat theory. Having examined the work of Mr. Dawkins, it is really clear to me that Dawkins has made zero contribution to the religion of evolutionism. Mr. Dawkins has however, made great strides in preaching his religion. Is evolutionism really a religion? You decide for yourself. I would encourage you go to the Museum of Natural History in New York City on any given weekend and visit the Darwin exhibit. There you will see the devotees of the evolutionism religion thronging and obsessing over the wax figure of the great prophet of their religion with all the charismatic, religious fervor of a snake handler.

Make no mistake, evolutionism is a religion, a religion requiring great faith. Wouldn't Mr. Dawkins love to be enshrined as a great thinker that opened our minds to his religion by getting people to reject the clear evidence of divine design? Dawkins needs to come up with at least one good scientific discovery or maybe a neat theory. Dawkins has contributed nothing to the advancement of his religion; no big banging cosmic boom, no dirt soup turning into people, no imaginary geologic column, no bogus radiometric dating methods, no Piltdown hoax, no Lucy hoax, nothing. Richard Dawkins has contributed zilch to the religion of evolutionism, except of course God bashing, this is the only thing that Richard Dawkins has had to offer his religion. If I were Dawkins, I certainly would not hold my breath waiting to be enshrined into any of evolutionism's temples as one of the great thinking prophets of the religion. God bashing simply is not a scientific achievement.

Sagan Studied the Prophets?

In chapter one of his delusional book, Dawkins would go on to quote Carl Sagan from his book *Pale Blue Dot*. Lets read the quote:

How is it that hardly any major religion has looked at the science and concluded, ' This is better than we thought! The universe is much bigger than our prophets said, grander, more subtle, more elegant'? Instead they say, 'No, no, no! My God is a little god, and I want him to stay that way.' A religion, old or new, that stressed the magnificence of the Universe as revealed by modern science might be able to draw forth reserves of reverence and awe hardly tapped by the conventional faiths.

On a more comical note, I simply must comment on the paragraph that follows the quote by Carl Sagan, Dawkins writes:

Consequently, I hear myself often described as a religious man. An American student wrote to me that she had asked her professor whether he had a view about me. 'Sure' he replied. 'He's positive science is incompatible with religion, but he waxes ecstatic about nature and the universe. To me that is religion!'

Regarding the quotation by Mr. Dawkins, mentioning the unnamed student and her unnamed professor, Dawkins is downplaying his religious involvement, while at the same time stroking his own ego. Dawkins' religion is clearly not waxing ecstatic over nature or the universe. Waxing is not what Dawkins is obsessed with, nor is science his obsession. His obsession is dethroning the Creator. Dawkins attempts to accomplish this by pedaling the evolutionism religion.

We all know that when you tell a child that a frog can turn into a prince, the kid clearly understands that they are hearing a fairytale. Oh, if the evolutionist only had the common sense of a toddler, I would not be writing this book. It takes many years of repetitious conditioning to get adults to accept what even a child knows is clearly nonsense. Prophets of evolutionism have such great faith that they believe that a dot, that's right a dot, exploded, creating all of the galaxies, and then dirt turned into a bacteria that would eventually turn into a human. In the next chapter you will see why that is not only unlikely but totally impossible. No Richard, its not the waxing ecstatic about nature and the universe that would constitute your religion, as if Dawkins ever waxed ecstatic pondering anything. Its Dawkins' faith in the unproven and the disprovable that would constitute his religion. Labeling one's self a deep thinker simply does not make it so. Now I will get back to the quote by Carl Sagan. I just could not resist chasing that *"waxes ecstatic"* rabbit. I felt that we could use a little comic relief.

Now back to addressing the quote by Carl Sagan, *"the universe is much bigger than our prophets said"*.

I challenge anyone to show me a quote from the King James Version of the Bible that is not compatible with science. I happen to have a few quotes from the prophets. Here are several of many quotes that could have advanced the progress of science thousands of years ahead of it's time. Carl Sagan clearly had no idea what the prophets said.

It is He who sits above the circle of the earth, And its inhabitants are like grasshoppers, Who stretches out the heavens like a curtain, And spreads them out like a tent to dwell in. Isaiah 40:22 NKJV

The prophet is saying that the earth is round. He wrote this thousands of years ago, while "enlightened scientists" believed the earth was flat, but would later learn that the earth is round like the prophet Isaiah had been saying. This strongly suggests that today's modern "scientists" would have been flat earthers, ignorantly believing that science is incompatible with the scriptures. This is but one of many examples of the prophets being right and "enlightened scientists" being wrong. For the life of me, I just cannot envision a small God stretching out the heavens like a curtain.

When the morning stars sang together, and all the sons of God shouted for joy?
Job 38:7 NKJV

Asteroseismology (stellar seismology) could be summed up as the interpretation of the frequency spectra of stars. It is very interesting to me that scientists can now record symphonic music from the stars through high powered telescopic observation. Scientists believe that the pulsation of the stars is causing the frequencies. The stars are actually delivering brilliantly composed music, try to fathom that. An article ran in the BBC News on October, 23, 2008 by Pallab Ghosh. The article is entitled '*Team Records Music From Stars*'. This is so incredible, "enlightened scientists" are just now figuring out what God was conveying to Job some 5,000 years ago.

By what way is the light parted, which scattereth the east wind upon the earth?
Job 38:24 KJV

The light from the sun heats the earth and causes the wind to blow. God conveyed this 5,000 years before "enlightened scientists" would figure it out. Anyone who has studied biblical prophets could not conclude that their teachings hinder science, on the contrary, they illuminate science. If Sagan had studied the prophets he would have had a better understanding of just how scientifically accurate the prophets were. My guess is that Sagan never studied the scriptures, but was in fact blowing smoke. The evolutionism religion is the greatest hindrance to science that there has ever been.

Therefore from one man, and him as good as dead, were born as many as the stars of the sky in multitude— innumerable as the sand which is by the seashore.
Hebrews 11:7 NKJV

The number of the stars in the sky compared with the innumerable grains of sand on the seashore. Seems to me the prophets had a great understanding of the infinite number of stars and thus the inconceivable magnitude of the cosmos, long before "enlightened scientists" knew it. Not until the 20th century were scientists aware of the number of stars, or aware of how unaware they are. Latest guesstimate puts it at about 20 trillion stars for each person on the planet. Not 20 trillion, but 20 trillion times 7 billion. That's a big number. I guess when the prophets called the stars innumerable, they knew exactly what they were talking about, but "enlightened scientists" would not get an inkling until the 20th century.

"Have you entered the springs of the sea? Or have you walked in the search of the depths?
Job 38:16 NKJV

Not until 1977 did scientists discover that there were springs at the bottom of the sea. Try to imagine that, subterranean water, beneath the seas. Who could have dreamed that? How could someone had known this 5,000 years ago? Perhaps God knew because He created everything in existence. God not only has all the answers, God is the answer.

"Can you bind the cluster of Pleiades, Or loose the belt of Orion? Job 38:31 NKJV

Astronomers have discovered that the star cluster of Orion is "loose", there is no gravitational pull effecting the star cluster. Pleiades on the hand, is bound by a gravitational force. So Pleiades is being bound by gravity, while the belt of Orion is loose. Perfectly consistent with God's declaration that was spoken to Job some 5,000 years before modern science would get a clue. Now how could God have possibly known these facts? Perhaps because He is God and He created the cosmos and everything that we can possibly see, ponder and study.

"You Lord, in the beginning laid the foundations of the earth. And the heavens are the work of Your hands. They will perish but You will remain: And they will grow old like a garment: Like a cloak You will fold them up, And they will be changed but you are the same, And Your years will not fail." Hebrews 1:10-12 NKJV

How would a *"little god"* fold up the heavens and earth and change them like a cloak? I will clear that up for Carl. God is not little, nor did the prophets ever imply that He is little, on the contrary, they declared His incomprehensible greatness. What Bible was Sagan reading anyway?

God thunders marvelously with His voice: He does great things which we cannot comprehend. Job 37:5 NKJV

Hmm, things we cannot comprehend. What's that mean? I will explain it for Carl Sagan. Carl, that means its deep. Beyond our grasp, without end, infinite, unfathomable. Your brain couldn't even begin to take a nibble of it. I hope that helps to clear up any of the Sagan confusion on the prophet's understanding of how great their Creator is.

Here we see that modern "scientists" are just now figuring out what the scriptures could have taught them thousands of years ago, had they believed their Creator, as opposed to the flat earthers. Carl Sagan clearly did not know what the prophets said about their God. Carl was either spouting his ignorance or he was a liar. Perhaps Sagan believed that by distorting the true record, he could some how make the religion of evolutionism seem possible. Science is perfectly compatible with the teachings of the biblical prophets. Science is totally incompatible with the religion of evolutionism. Sorry, I don't make the rules. Was Sagan deliberately lying? I am not sure. I do know with all certainty that the deceased Carl Sagan now believes beyond all doubt that there is a Creator, an awesome Creator.

To marvel over the complexities of a plant cell and the universe that is within, is not to dismiss the sheer indescribable magnitude of the cosmos. To deny the signature of a Designer on either would not only be absurd, but would require pure, blind religious faith. Sagan was claiming that the cosmos have been revealed by modern science. No Carl, the scriptures are, in reality, being verified by modern science. The prophets were scientifically accurate about everything that "enlightened scientists" would not figure out until thousands of years later.

Chapter Two

The Evolution Hypothesis

Dawkins Understands Essentially How Life Began

The following is a verbatim quote from Richard Dawkins during the God Delusion Debate in Birmingham, Alabama - October, 2007 :

"We now understand essentially how life came into being. We know that we are all cousins of all animals and plants. We know that we are descendant from a common ancestor which might have been something like bacteria. We know the process by which that came about. We don't know the details but we understand essentially how it came about. There are still gaps in our understanding. We don't understand how the cosmos came into existence in the first place but we're working on that. The scientific enterprise is an active seeking, an active seeking out of gaps in our knowledge, seeking out of ignorance so that we can work to plug that ignorance. But religion teaches us to be satisfied with not really under-standing. Every one of these difficult questions that come up, science says right, let's roll up our sleeves and work on it. Religion says oh, God did it." - Richard Dawkins

Does Dawkins really understand essentially how life came into existence? Dawkins is saying that he essentially understands organic evolution (origin of life by spontaneous generation); however, there is no evidence that organic evolution has ever taken place. It just has not happened. It is not provable, it is not science, it is faith. For Dawkins to claim that he understands organic evolution is a demonstration of his willingness to mislead people in an attempt to sell his religion. What huge religious faith Dawkins has to believe in something unproven and improvable and then go as far as to claim that he understands it.

Does Dawkins really know we are cousins with all plants and animals? Such a belief could not possibly be derived from scientific observation. Plants require carbon dioxide, animals require oxygen. We have a serious chicken and egg dilemma here. Which came first and how did one survive without the other? Certainly a deep thinker like Dawkins would have made this consideration. The symbiotic relationship between plants and animals render the possibility of them being related to each other non-existent. Again, Dawkins demonstrates his blind religious faith in things unproven, improvable and even impossible.

Does Dawkins really believe there are gaps in his understanding? Well, that's a relief, I was afraid we didn't agree on anything; but, I can certainly agree that there are gaps in Dawkins' understanding. Come on now Richard, you claim to be a great thinker that thinks for himself, so think about this... Has organic evolution ever been proven? Has macro evolution ever been proven? Has chemical evolution ever been proven? Has stellar evolution ever been proven? Has cosmic evolution ever been proven? Since you seem to be in the dark on these matters, I will clear things up for you. The answer to all of these questions is no. In fact, the scientific evidence points to the contrary. These forms of evolution are unproven and improvable. They are in fact disprovable and only digestible within the blind religious faith of evolutionism.

Dawkins' quote also says, *"We don't know how the cosmos came into existence in the first place, but we're working on it."* Since Dawkins does not even know what his religion teaches about the origin of the cosmos, I will be glad to enlighten him. You see Richard, *"20 billion years ago, a dot, no bigger than the period at the end of this sentence"* spun around and around until it exploded, forming the galaxies and the innumerable stars that exist today. That Richard, is how the cosmos came into existence, if you believe that the evolutionism religion is science. Dawkins should have a better grasp on his own world view. *"Filling ignorance"* with unproven and improvable fantasies will never constitute science; but this practice fits perfectly into the definition of blind religious faith. The religion of evolutionism requires more faith than any other religion. A frog is never going to turn into a prince no matter how much time you give it, and no matter how many hits of acid one drops on a given weekend. Such transformations may take place in fairytales, but do not happen in reality. Such transformations only take place in the imagination or perhaps a hallucination.

This is the end of the Dawkins quote *"Everyone of these difficult questions that comes up, science says right, let's roll up our sleeves and work on it. Religion says oh God did it."* So, how does the religion of evolutionism work on it? How does the religion of evolutionism respond to these difficult questions? By fabricating hoaxes, filling textbooks with lies and asking students to "just imagine" evolutionary transformations taking place. Evolutionism is in no way science or scientific, evolutionism is very much a religion.

Is There Reason to Hypothesize Evolution?

Let's examine six actual definitions of evolution. We will begin with cosmic evolution because this theory is the book of Genesis in the religion of evolutionism. These definitions define six forms of evolution. My source is *The Creation Series* by Dr. Kent Hovind, founder of CSE (Creation Science Evangelism). The seminar style DVD presentation is a powerful, informative and captivating eye opener that I highly recommend. You can find this DVD series at **www. drdino.com**. If you refuse to be persuaded by faith, you will be persuaded by scientific facts.

1. *Cosmic evolution - Origin of time, space and matter.*

If you will recall, 20 billion years ago a spinning dot exploded, vomiting up the cosmos. This fantasy has no scientific merit whatsoever. This theory, which is taught to children as fact, is pure dung. Sorry, but that's the nicest thing I can say about it because of the absolute scientific facts that make this "theory" impossible. Let's start with the law of conservation of angular momentum, meaning that when a spinning object explodes or breaks apart, all of the objects that fly off will be spinning in the same direction, conserving angular momentum. Well Richard, you have a problem, you see all of our planets and their moons do not spin in the same direction. Some spin clock wise, others spin counter clockwise. Astronomers have even discovered galaxies that spin counter clockwise. This kind of puts a damper on the exploding, spinning dot theory doesn't it Richard? Next, why is the sun composed almost entirely of hydrogen and helium, while planet earth is not even one percent hydrogen and helium? Didn't they come out of the same big bang? One would think that the earth and sun would share similar elemental compositions if they came from the same bang. I would think a deep thinker like Dawkins would have caught that. Furthermore, at the rate our sun is burning up cubic tons of hydrogen; 600 million cubic tons of hydrogen per second, the sun would have been so big 4 billion years ago that it would have incinerated the neighboring planets. Thus, science reveals that this universe cannot possibly be 4.6 billion years old. Science also tells us that the earth and the sun could not possibly have emerged from the same exploding bang. We can easily conclude that cosmic evolution is in no way science, cosmic evolution is religion.

2. Stellar evolution - Origin of the stars and planets

Stellar evolution has never been observed. No one has ever seen a star form. We do see stars burn out. We see stars explode, this is observable. Stars will nova or supernova leaving behind nova rings, however, no one has ever seen a star form or be born. At the rate these stars explode (about every 30 years) we have enough of these nova rings to account for about 6,000 years of time. Perhaps these nova rings disappear after a few thousand years, yet the rings around Saturn can last for billions of years? Do you see how ridiculous the evolutionist has to become to cling to this theory? Still there is no record of any star ever forming itself. Why is that do you suppose? Perhaps because stars do not create themselves. Stars die and we have scientific evidence for that, but there is zero evidence that a star has ever created itself. Stellar evolution has no scientific merit and only takes place in the imagination. Stellar evolution is not science, stellar evolution is religion.

3. *Chemical evolution - Origin of higher elements from hydrogen.*

We need the stars to make the elements and we need the elements to make the stars. We have another chicken and egg dilemma. Which appeared first? Did the stars make the elements or did the elements make the stars? This does not add up to anyone who is thinking scientifically. Who in their right scientific mind could believe that uranium evolved from hydrogen? Elements like iron, carbon or uranium could not possibly have evolved from hydrogen. Such elements could only have been created. This fantasy of higher elements evolving from hydrogen has never been observed, it is not testable, and it is not science. Where did the hydrogen that all of the elements evolved from, come from? The spinning dot? I do not mean to go out of my way to insult Mr. Dawkins, but nor shall I don kid gloves when addressing the blind faith required to believe that all of the elements in the periodic table evolved from hydrogen. Chemical evolution is not science, chemical evolution is religion.

4. *Organic evolution - Origin of life*

Non-living matter does not spring to life by spontaneous generation. This has never been observed in science. Organic evolution is unproven and improvable; however, it is still taught as fact in textbooks. *"Life must have emerged in this pre biotic soup"* (it just *"must have"*). Waiter, there's a fly in my soup! Mud soup does not manufacture living organisms, it never has and never will. The synthesizing of cells is no doubt on the genetic engineering horizon. This could have huge benefits in the practice of medicine. Unfortunately, it could also have huge implications in genetically altering humans, or perhaps new diseases that could drastically reduce the human population, and in the hands of Darwinian mad men, that is a creepy probability. The closer researchers get to this possibility, the more evident the signature of a highly complex Designer becomes. For decades many researchers have been working hard, studying, learning, struggling, and spending millions of dollars to advance this cause. I would call that a major intelligent directing process. I think it's safe to say that mud could not synthesize, much less create a living cell. Could the successful synthesizing of a cell make a case for the spontaneous generation of life? Not hardly. Suppose you managed to successfully copy a book, would that mean that the original copy did not have an author? No, that would mean that major intelligent direction and persistence brought that copy into existence. This does not equate to mud soup springing to life. To synthesize a genome and use it to create a cell driven entirely by the synthetic genome is not organic evolution. This is replication of information already in existence. If scientists can boast that they have created a copy of a cell, then why would anyone conclude that the original cell was not created? To believe that rain on rocks over millions of years created mud soup that would produce living organisms would still require blind religious faith.

5. *Macro evolution - Changing from one species into another species*

Macro evolution has never been observed, not in reality, and not in any fossil record. When bones are dug up from the dirt, all anyone can honestly be certain of is that these bones are from a man or an animal that is no longer living. You cannot prove that these bones gave birth to a different species. There is zero evidence for macro evolution in any bones that have been uncovered. I understand the Piltdown hoax and the Lucy hoax exist, and more hoaxes will surely come. The evolutionists pedal their faith, they preach a hoax until it is totally exposed as a fraud. After slowly letting go of the hoax over decades they will latch on to a new and improved hoax. Textbooks will even publish these hoaxes decades after they have been exposed as fraudulent. If macro evolution were true, there would be an endless variety of intermediate species in the fossils. Darwinian "science" is desperate for anything to sell the religion of evolutionism to young minds. Since true evidence does not exist, fabricated "evidence" is presented as fact and called "science". Some textbooks even go as far as to ask the student to try to imagine a transformation taking place. Of all the religions, evolutionism has got to be the most ridiculous of them all. For 40 years the Piltdown man was taught in the public schools as fact, the missing link between apes and man. It was a hoax, an ape's jaw had been filed down to fit into a human skull. Molds of this were sent to science centers around the world. Universities never got anything but the molds from this hoax. Prophets of evolutionism will go to great lengths to fool the public, and sell their ideology, but in all fairness that is pretty typical of most religions.

6. *Micro evolution - Variations within a species*

Should micro evolution even be called evolution? It is actually a variation within a kind. Dogs can be bred to produce many different types of dogs; but, they always produce dogs. Micro evolution would be more accurately called variations within a kind. The reason that the priests of evolutionism have labeled these variations as micro evolution is done an effort to make the fantasy forms of evolution seem possible. You see ladies and gentlemen, you can breed a horse and a zebra and get something that looks a little like both, and there you have it, proof that your grandpa is a monkey. Horses and zebras are of the same kind. If the religion of evolutionism calls them different species and their offspring yet a new species, does that mean your grandpa is an ape or bacteria? Hardly, that means that the animals are of the same kind (able to interbreed) and that they are called different species and the offspring yet another type of species so that the ridiculous idea of macro evolution will seem possible to the religiously indoctrinated mind. It is observed that a donkey and a horse will produce a mule, and that mule is infertile 95% of the time. Does this prove that a bacteria spawned a sponge or that a dinosaur laid a bird egg? Does this prove that a chimp gave birth to a human (one of each gender in the same location and generation)? There is zero evidence that one kind of animal has ever changed into another kind of animal. To believe that you share a common heritage with cockroaches and jelly fish requires pure religious faith.

Richard Dawkins' whole religious faith hinges on the idea that all of these forms of evolution are possible. Well, we now know that science has proven the impossibility of these fantasies. Dawkins is left with nothing but blind religious faith. Dawkins, being a thinking man, has to rely on billions of years and disprovable fantasies to remain faithful to his chosen religion. The origin of the cosmos (spin + dot = cosmos), and the origin of life (dirt soup + lightning = life). These fantastic notions are scientifically disprovable. Dawkins has no real science to lean on that would warrant his allegiance to this religion. Dawkins has opted for blind religious faith in evolutionism and has chosen to ignore scientific facts.

The next time you get a chance, please pick up a rock. Hold that rock in your hand, look at it very closely and ask yourself... Is this rock my grandpa? Can you honestly answer yes to that question? Let's take it a step further, the next time you get a chance, pick up a speck of dust, no bigger than the period at the end of this sentence. Look at it very closely and then ask yourself... Is this tiny speck the mother of the rock that is my grandpa? If you are an evolutionist and you are feeling a tad moronic right now, it's understandable. Don't beat yourself up over it, we have all been repetitiously brainwashed. Just admit it; a speck did not give birth to a rock that is your grandpa. It took many, many years of repetitious conditioning to get us to believe something so ridiculous. It is time to release ourselves from these shackles of silliness.

The Intangible Geologic Column

Is there a 4 billion year old geologic column somewhere on planet earth? If you believe the typical science textbook, you would be left with the impression that there are layers of earth that date the different eras in the earth's history. This geologic column does indeed exist, but it is not tangible, it only exists in the textbooks and in the imaginations of "enlightened scientists". If there was a geologic column that was a billion years old, it would miles thick. The geologic column is pure fantasy. The earth does indeed have sedimentary layering, indicating rapid layering as a result of a huge flood. There is a whole variety of fossils that exist all throughout this layering. The fact that the fossils are even present should be clear evidence to a scientist of a rapid burial, because we know that fossils are formed by rapid burial in mineral rich material, with water present. The rapid burial of organisms inside of rapidly layering sediment is not evidence of a billion year process. Why am I even forced to debunk this fantasy? Why? Because we have been brainwashed. If there were millions of years in between each strata, then there would be erosion in between the layers, wouldn't there? If these strata's were different ages, then why would upside down trees be running through millions of years of strata? An upside down tree running through multiple layers can point to only one possibility, and that is rapid layering in the event of a great flood. To get a good visual, go to the mall and find one of those glass panels filled with colored sand and water, shake it up, and watch the layers appear almost instantly. If this information is contrary to the beliefs that you hold about earth science, it should cause you to have one of two reactions. You will either feel enlightened or you will feel angry. If you are angry, that's because the geologic column has been debunked, shedding the light of truth on a fictitious fantasy. I urge you to get over any anger.

I must admit that I had been duped as well, so don't feel bad. If you are feeling enlightened, then this is a strong indicator that like me, you have a desire to get to the truth and not be a gullible victim of evolutionism.

There is ample scientific evidence that there was a world-wide flood about 4,400 years ago. The oldest tree on earth is 4,400 years old. The oldest coral reef is 4,400 years old. The oldest desert is 4,400 years old. At the rate that the oceans are getting saltier, due to minerals being washed in from rivers and streams, we can account for 4,400 years worth of salt in the oceans. The majority of earth's water was subterranean fresh water before this great flood, according to the evidence. The amount of salt in our oceans is perfectly consistent with the Genesis account of the earth's history, but highly inconsistent with an earth that is billions of years old.

Consider the Hovind theory. I will make my very best lame attempt to sum up this theory in just a few sentences. I will hardly even scratch the surface on the mountain of evidence and scientific facts that make the Hovind theory the most plausible. I first considered and started to study this most credible theory after being exposed to the theory in great detail on the previously mentioned Creation DVD Series, by CSE. This theory makes the most sense, not because it conforms to my faith, but because it conforms to science. It really is the only theory that has answers to all of my questions, refreshingly, answers that are backed by reality science.

The majority of water in this global flood did not come from rain, but was the result of subterranean water chambers bursting forth, just like the Bible say. The earth was much different prior to the flood, probably the majority of the earth was covered by land with lush, dense, tropical vegetation.

A huge impact caused the subterranean water chambers to burst out of what we now know as fault lines. The force behind this water and rock would have been so tremendous that it would have carried the water and rock well into space, explaining why we have rocks and water in space, and why the moon shows clear evidence of having been peppered by rocks.

Something like a meteor struck the earth, knocking it to its 23 degree tilt. The earth's wobble from this impact is still being measured today, although the wobble is almost gone, scientists know that something struck the earth with an enormous impact about 4,400 years ago. Likely it was a meteor and it would have broken through an ice canopy that enveloped the earth prior to the great flood. That ice canopy would have been suspended high in the atmosphere. This ice canopy gave the earth it's hyper baric chamber effect that allowed for long life spans and the enormous plants and animals. This canopy would have also filtered harmful radiation from space. Again this theory is consistent with the Genesis account and with reality science.

The falling ice canopy buried mammoths standing upright with food in their mouths. The mammoths were entombed by -300 degree ice, but at no time has the temperature on earth ever been as low as -300 degrees. Ice from the upper limits of the earth's atmosphere would have been -300 degrees. That's why the mammoths were buried and frozen so quickly. Mammoths were not cold weather animals, they were elephants and not living in an arctic region, nor were the jungle cats that were buried along with them. Movies like *Ice Age,* are simply fiction but can be used as great propaganda techniques for conditioning young minds.

The collapse of this huge ice firmament would have caused an ice age, but this ice age lasted for a matter of years, dozens at the most, not millions of years. This ice canopy is consistent with the Genesis account and with true science. There was no record of short life spans or cold weather seasons recorded in Genesis prior to this great catastrophic event. This is consistent with an earth that did not have a 23 degree tilt, but did have an ice firmament creating a hyper baric chamber effect that would benefit the plants and animals living on the earth. This fits perfectly into the Genesis account and is also perfectly compatible with science. There would have been huge plants, animals and men having long life spans in the highly oxygenated, hyper baric chamber that was the pre flood world. This is how the 80 ton braceosaurus could get their needed oxygen through nostrils the size of a horse's nostrils. This is consistent with the scientific evidence of huge plants and animals that existed in the pre flood world. The science textbooks will not mention the 12 foot skeletons of men that have been unearthed, because it works against their evolution theory, but many such skeletons do exist.

There is powerful evidence that there was a great global flood just about 4,400 years ago. So how did land resurface? Fair enough question. The enormous weight of all this water would eventually cause the earth beneath the weight to buckle and sink down, as the water pushed one portion of the earth down, an equal and opposite reaction would be causing land to rise up, and mountains to form elsewhere. This is why so many mountains show evidence of this, clearly crinkled, pushed into position. This is why clam shells exists at the highest peaks of Mount Everest. All of the land in the world was under water about 4,400 years ago. This is perfectly consistent with the Genesis account, and this is also perfectly consistent with real science.

Please don't get upset with me because evidence for a geologic column that is billions of years old is absent, while the evidence of a worldwide flood is present. I did not make up the rules, I simply examined the evidence. Maybe, just maybe there is a reason that close to 300 cultures have recorded legends of a catastrophic global flood taking place, with a family of survivors aboard a huge ark filled with animals.

I assume that anyone reading this book has two parents, four grandparents, eight great grandparents and so on. Realize that only two hundred years ago there were less than a billion people on planet earth, and that two thousand years ago there were less than 250 million people on earth. We have seen the human population go from a quarter billion to almost 8 billion in two thousand years. So if man has been on this earth for millions of years, then why are there not trillions of humans on the earth? Perhaps because mankind has not been on this earth for millions of years. So I ask you to just keep doubling that number of grandparents for every generation, and you will eventually discover that you are related to the whole world. If you do a little math you will discover that the earth's human population likely started from just a handful of people about 4,400 years ago. Isn't that interesting?

Scientific Dating methods

Astronomical dating

If we see star light from millions of light years away, that proves that the stars are millions of years old. It is fair for one to reason that, since we can see star light, then the stars must have been there for millions of years. I do not agree. According to one of Einstein's theories, the speed of light is constant at 186,000 miles per second. I believe that Einstein was wrong on this one. For Einstein to know this with certainty, he would have had to have been present to measure the speed of light since the very first light. It is just a theory and we know that theories are not established laws but hypothesized. Now you will not likely read this in a science textbook, but many scientists believe in a Euclidean universe, where energy, matter and time are normal, not relative to a constant speed of light. So light's velocity is not necessarily constant. Light could have traveled 100 million times faster than the speed that it now travels at some point since the creation. Who can be sure, since there is no scientific evidence that makes this theory any less plausible than Einstein's? My thought is, if all forms of energy are subject to change, then why would light be any different? I believe at some point light moved millions of times faster than what we are measuring it at today. I would also like to add that God created man in a mature state, so it is not too much of a stretch for me to believe that He is wise enough to provide star light at the time of the creation. God can create stars, I am sure that getting light from point A to point B would not pose too much of a challenge. God can create light, even light that is millions of light years in length. The Creator would only have to say *"let there be light"* and there would be light.

Dating by radiometric decay methods

Fossils and rocks cannot be dated as millions of years old by any radiometric decay methods. For one, radiometric dating is not proven scientifically. Furthermore, validity investigations have proven time and again that radiometric dating is a fraud, you won't read that in your science textbook, but it's a fact. We just have to take their word for it because they are scientists, and scientists are right about everything. Let's not be so gullible. Geologic strata were given their fabricated dates and ages long before radiometric dating was ever thought up or experimented with. If someone claims that they know the age of a layer of strata or of a fossil within to be millions of years old, by radiometric decay methods, that person is either lying or ignorant. Radiometric dating is not a valid process for determining the age of any rock or bone to be millions of years old, it simply does not work, and would depend on the geologic column being true. So we know that the strata is billions of years old because of radiometric dating, and we know that radiometric dating works because the strata is billions of years old. Sadly, evolutionism has to depend on that dreaded circular reasoning to make their case. Keep in mind, radiometric dating was employed well over 100 years after the intangible geologic column that "proves its accuracy" was even fabricated.

Dating methods are based on 3 unprovable and questionable assumptions:

1. That the rate of decay has been constant throughout time.

2. That the isotope abundances in the specimen date have not been altered during its history by addition or removal of either parent or daughter isotopes.

3. That when the rock first formed it contained a known amount of daughter material.

We must realize that past processes may not be occurring at all today, and that some may have occurred at rates and intensities far different from a similar process today.

Radioisotopes and the Age of the Earth;
Larry Vardiman, Andrew Snelling, Eugene Chaffin; Chapter 1

    A group of renown scientists started a research project in 1997. The group was called the RATE group. RATE being an acronym for Radioisotopes and the Age of The Earth. This group of scientists would spend eight years doing research on this project. These researchers concluded that the use of carbon 14 dating to determine the age of fossils to be millions of years old could have only been done by mistake or by fraud, because the half life of 14C is only 5,730 years. This research team included the following scientists.

Larry Vardiman, PhD Atmospheric Science
Russell Humphreys, PhD Physics
Eugene Chaffin, PhD Physics
John Baumgardner, PhD Geophysics
Donald DeYoung, PhD Physics
Steven Austin, PhD Geology
Andrew Snelling, PhD Geology
Steven Boyd, PhD Hebraic and Cognate Studies

Samples were taken from ten different coal layers that, according to evolutionists, represent different time periods in the geologic column (Cenozoic, Mesozoic, and Paleozoic). The RATE group obtained these samples from the U.S. Department of Energy Coal Sample Bank, from samples collected from major coalfields across the United States. The chosen coal samples, which dated millions to hundreds of millions of years old based on standard evolution time estimates, all contained measurable amounts of 14C. In all cases, careful precautions were taken to eliminate any possibility of contamination from other sources. Samples, in all three "time periods", displayed significant amounts of 14C. This is a significant discovery. Since the half-life of 14C is relatively short (5,730 years), there should be no detectable 14C after about 100,000 years. The average 14C estimated age for all three layers from these three time periods was approximately 50,000 years. However, using a more realistic pre-flood 14C / 12C ratio reduces that age to about 5,000 years.

Mike Riddle *Carbon-14 radiometric-dating rate*

    I pulled this excerpt from the website answersingenesis.org . I understand that the evolutionist that is faithfully devoted to their religion, is going to grasp at potassium-argon, uranium, and lead dating methods to fabricate their preconceived beliefs of millions or billions of years. When a technique for "proving millions of years" is exposed as bogus, the evolutionist will scramble to other improvable techniques for determining millions of years. The evolutionist is embracing a fantasy. Investigations into the accuracy and validity of these outlandish claims have proven these techniques to be fraudulent time and time again. Rocks and fossils being millions of years old could never be proven in a court of law. The evolutionists have to fabricate data to sell their lie of billions of years. There is no dating method that can consistently date any fossil to be millions of years old. This should be an indicator to a scientist that the evolutionary dating methods are either flawed or fraudulent. Do you have a question that you believe would stump the creationist? If so, please visit **answersingenesis.org** for a detailed and explanatory answer to that question.

Dating by appearance

Fossils and rocks in geologic strata simply cannot be dated by their appearance, anyone who claims that they can be dated this way is either ignorant or lying. Think of it, you pick up a chicken wing bone from the KFC parking lot, you look at it and then decide that it is exactly three weeks old. I think we can agree that this notion is ridiculous. Miraculously, one dedicated to Charles Lyell's geologic column fantasy can pick up a bone, look at it, and decide that it is 100 million years old. The age of a bone simply cannot be honestly determined by its appearance. No one could possibly know the age of any rock by simply looking at it, unless they were there when that rock was formed. *"We date the fossils by the layers"* ... *"We date the layers by the fossils"*, this is called circular reasoning, this is not science. T-Rex bones are found with marrow in them and soft tissue dino skin has even been discovered outside of ice. We can be certain that bones could not retain red blood cells for millions of years, hundreds maybe. Thousands? That's stretching it, but millions? NO WAY!

Enlightened paleontologists were so duped into believing that dinosaur bones looked millions of years old, that they did not even bother having these bones examined for evidence of blood cells. Now that the evidence of red blood cells in dino bones is public, the paleontologists, religiously devoted to the fictitious geologic column, will scratch their heads and ponder how those red blood cells lasted for all those millions of years. Now, if one is so dedicated to their religion that they believe that the red blood cells remained for 70 million years, then I must admire their religious faith. Maybe, just maybe the dragon legends in every culture with pictures of heroes slaying T-rex in their art work, and even on their coins, maybe all of that is just a product of fantasy... Or perhaps someone believing that red blood cells can last 70 million years is the one who is duped by fantasy. Will the real delusion please stand up?

Dating by location

Rocks and bones cannot be dated by their location or their depth in geologic strata. Interestingly, evolutionists will tell us that they date the layer of strata by the fossils that they find in that layer, and then they will tell us that they date the fossils by the layer of strata that they came from. Which is it? There is no answer for this question. This is circular reasoning and anyone claiming to be a real scientist should have enough sound judgment to abandon circular reasoning as a method for determining billions of years. When fossils of organisms that are used to date geologic strata that is "millions of years old" are discovered alive and well on planet earth, like the lobe finned fish, graftolite, or trilobite, evolutionists will scratch their head and ponder how that organism survived all those millions of years. They could never question the validity of their sacred geologic column. They could never reason that if an organism is still alive today, then in all fairness, it cannot be used as an index fossil to date any strata. Why let facts get in the way of such a great religion?

Fundamental Problems:
As we study the fossil record, we come upon a variety of very serious problems which undermine the strata / fossil theory. Three of the most important are these:

1.) At the very bottom of all the strata (the geologic column) is the Cambrian strata, which is filled with complex, multi celled life. This is termed the "Cambrian explosion" of sudden life forms all at once.
2.) There are no transitional species throughout the column. This problem is also called fossil gaps or missing links.

3.) Mixed-up and out-of-order strata are regularly found.

Singly or together they destroy the evolutionary argument from the rock strata.

The Evolution Handbook, page 436 Vance Ferrell

Facts, not Fluff

The *Evolution Handbook* by Vance Ferrell was formerly entitled *The Evolution Cruncher.* I highly recommend this book because you get almost 1,000 pages of facts, not fluff, for about 5 bucks. This is an amazing deal because this book will arm you with scientific facts that dismantle any case for evolutionism that may be presented to you as science. The subject index in the book makes finding and referencing these scientific facts quick and easy. Over 3,000 scientific facts that totally discredit evolutionism. This book covers all of the topics that are used to make a case for evolutionism. Now, if you are dedicated to evolutionism because of religious or spiritual reasons, then the book may not help your understanding. Some people will avoid the truth, they want to bury their head in the sand. If they can just ignore the facts, then they don't have to consider possibilities within the boundaries of reality. Now, if your true desire is to consider science and look at scientific data, weighing all of the information to reach your conclusions, then you really need a copy of the *Evolution Handbook.* This book just obliterates every single leg that evolutionism attempts to stand on, from the topics of abiogenesis to the zoogenesis theory and everything in between. If every college student had a copy of the *Evolution Handbook* by Vance Ferrel, their professors would be left speechless. You can get these books for like five bucks a copy. I believe that if you buy in bulk for the purpose of arming youth with the truth, you can get these books for even less. What a great gift to give a young person heading off to college. I got my copy at **drdino.com** and I just love it.

Chapter Three

Does God Exist?

Driven by "Improbability"

We can now safely say that the illusion of design in living creatures is just that - an illusion. -Richard Dawkins, *The God Delusion.*

B ad news ladies and gentlemen, all the impression of design is just an illusion. The good news is that Dawkins has evolved to the point that his powers of observation have penetrated the fog of this illusion, so now we no longer need to trust what we can see with our own two eyes. Now we can safely place our faith, and our eternal destinies into the all knowing mind of an enlightened scientist, who has declared the visual evidence for design to be an illusion. The central case for Dawkins' book, *The God Delusion* can be summed up with his idea that God is improbable. Dawkins' denial of a Creator is not based on scientific facts, but on what Dawkins perceives as an improbability. His whole case is admittedly, just his guess that the idea of a Creator seems *"highly improbable indeed"*. Well, since you put it that way, then it sounds kind of smart and I guess I should believe it.

I can just envision Dawkins with his thumb and index finger caressing his chin, as if to be submerged deep in thought, while offering us his insightful wisdom, *"highly improbable indeed"*. Ben Stein, in his search for some hard scientific data backing Dawkins' improbability of a God declaration, asked Dawkins to give us some scientific figures for his conclusions, and this is Dawkins' reply;

Dawkins -   *"Well it's hard to put a figure on it, but, but, I, I, I'd put it at something like 99% against it."*

Stein -   *"How do you know its 99% and not say, 97%?"*

Dawkins -   *"You asked me to put a figure on it and I, I am not comfortable putting a figure on it. I think its, I just think its very unlikely."*

Stein -   *"Why? That you couldn't put a number on it like 49%?"*

Dawkins -   *"No of course not. Well, well, I think it would be, I think its unlikely, but, but its quite far from 50%."*

From the documentary movie, *Expelled, No Intelligence Allowed* - Ben Stein

Now, who would have the audacity to question mathematical probabilities of hard science as concrete as this? Dawkins is not only trying to convince his audience that a Creator is *"highly improbable indeed"*, but he has backed these assertions with this rock solid scientific evidence, telling us that he guesses creation is 99% unlikely. What a great scientific breakthrough. Is this the evidence that drives Dawkins into his anti-God rants? I don't think so. There must be more. Let's dig deeper.

A true scientist, understanding that there are infinite mysteries in the universe, would never totally discount any given possibility based on a ratio of 99 to 1 odds against that possibility (supposing that the percentile were factual, and not just pulled out of the thin air, as Dawkins obviously did). In the field of science, one percent is a pretty big cause for consideration, I would think. These kinds of odds are beaten on a daily basis. The odds that point to creation are insurmountable, as we will soon discover. Let us probe the mind of evolutionary thought. After reading chapters three and four, you can safely conclude that this delusion of Richard Dawkins' is just that - a delusion.

Laws of Thermodynamics

First Law of Thermodynamics:
Energy or matter can be changed from one form to another, but it cannot be created or destroyed. The total amount of energy in the universe remains constant, it changes from one form to another (conservation).

How is it that any credentialed scientist, like Dawkins, could have overlooked the first law of thermodynamics? If energy is not created or destroyed and energy is always conserved, merely changing from one form to another, then how could the cosmos possibly have created itself from nothing? Such a simple question, with only one possible explanation. It is just not scientifically possible for all of the energy in the universe to have created itself from nothing. This leaves only one other possibility, the cosmos were created by a Creator. Naturalistic processes and billions of years do not create energy, time, space, matter or life. Since energy does exist, it must have originated outside of the known universe, with something non-physical as the cause.

Second Law of Thermodynamics:
In all energy exchanges, if no energy enters or leaves the system, the potential energy of the state will always be less than the original state (entropy).

Entropy, in nutshell, tells us that all structures and systems always tend toward disorder when left to themselves. That means that when reduced in any way they come from a point of having been more organized and more complex, not traceable to any big banging explosion or mud soup. If we could go back to the point when matter, space and time originated, the amount of energy needed to pull this off would exceed the total amount of energy in the universe, which would render this an impossibility according to the first law of thermodynamics. The second law of thermodynamics destroys any notion that matter can create itself, spring to life and then evolve into something more complex. To reason that plants and animals somehow spontaneously and simultaneously sprang into existence and then evolved in complexity is an impossibility when confronted by the laws of thermodynamics.

There is zero scientific evidence that any organism of any kind just sprang to life or has ever even evolved in complexity. I could expect an evolutionist to argue; What about bacteria becoming resistant to drugs, for example MRSA or VRE, they are getting smarter aren't they? No, they are not getting smarter and they are not getting more complex, they are in fact losing information. After bacteria is exposed to an antibiotic, their ribosomes can become deformed and being deformed the antibiotic can no longer latch on to the ribosome, making the bacteria resistant to the drug. This is in no way due to a gain of information, and this is not an increase in complexity. This resistance to drugs is actually due to a loss in complexity. Bacteria do not evolve into something smarter or more complex. There is zero scientific evidence that non-living matter has ever turned itself into a living organism. There is zero evidence that any organism has ever had an increase in complexity.

Radiohalos

Pleochroic halos, commonly referred to as radiohalos, are the rings left inside of a solid rock, like granite, as a result of radiation emissions from a radioactive particle. Today scientists find radiohalos from Polonium 210, 214 and 218 by the trillions inside of solid granite. The phenomena could not possibly take place in molten magma, which quickly dismisses the silly evolutionary notion that the earth started out as a huge blob of lava. The phenomena can only occur inside of solid rock, and that solid rock would had to have taken just a few minutes to form, because the half-life of Polonium 218 is under three minutes. The radiohalo is developed in less than a few minutes. The Polonium radiohalos just had to be brought into existence at the same time as the rock. That is amazing. The existence of granite, provably, came about in seconds, not billions of years. This is true of all the granite, from all over the world. It is very rare to find any Uranium 238 halos accompanying the Polonium halos, this quickly dismisses the idea that perhaps Polonium somehow evolved from Uranium (which evolved from Hydrogen, lol).

Just as Alka-Seltzer bubbles quickly disappear from a glass of water, they would even more quickly disappear if the Alka-Seltzer were somehow dropped into a large pool of red-hot molten magma deep in the earth. Now, is there a way that bubbles in the Alka-Seltzer water could be retained? It would be hard to do, but it could be done if the glass of water with the bubbles were immediately dipped into liquid nitrogen, which is very cold. The water would freeze almost instantly and the bubbles would remain captured. Robert V. Gentry *Creation's Tiny Mystery*

When Robert V. Gentry published his findings, his funding for research was immediately cut off. Evolutionism has zero tolerance for findings that prove a Creator. Like bubbles in the water being rapidly frozen into position, polonium radio-halos left inside of solid granite could only be present if the granite formed super fast or instantly. This simply does not fit into the evolutionary theory of the planet's origin. These findings fit perfectly into the creation theory. Here we have what is obviously clear evidence for the finger prints of a Creator bringing into existence His creation. It may have taken only an instant, but it couldn't have taken more than just a few minutes; it's just not scientifically possible that it could have taken millions or billions of years. Granite is unique, if you melt it down you will never be able turn it back into granite again. Scientists are clueless as to how it could have been formed, all they know for sure is that it was made real fast and there is lots of it. There is clear scientific evidence that granite was created in seconds, by a Creator, not over billions of years, this is an indisputable scientific fact. Why let science get in the way of such a great religion?

Atheists founded America?

Where did that come from? By saying America, Dawkins is referring to the United States of America. I am reasonably certain that the Pilgrims were not atheists, nor were the Puritans that would arrive later. The commonwealths that they established were Bible based. I guess, like Hitler, Dawkins believes, *"If you tell a lie long enough, and loud enough, people will believe it"*. Now, a more intelligent approach to try to strip the credit for the founding of the United States away from people with faith in Christ would have been to credit the union of the original colonies to Sir Francis Bacon. Sadly for Dawkins, Bacon was not even an atheist. Bacon had cultic Rosicrucian visions of a new Atlantis and a new world order. Strangely, Bacon had great foreknowledge of flying machines and weapons of mass destruction taking part in the process of establishing this new world order. Rosicrucians are considered by many experts to be a brotherhood, if not the mother of the Freemasons. Freemasonry had a huge influence on uniting the colonies to form the US government.

Many writers have sought to discover a close connection between the Rosicrucians and the Freemasons, and some, indeed have advanced the theory that the latter are only the successes of the former. Whether this opinion is correct or not, there are sufficient coincidences of character between the two to render history of Rosicrucianism highly interesting to the Masonic student. Albert G. Mackey, *Encyclopedia of Freemasonry, Volume II* page 639

When Dawkins implies in his book that Washington and Jefferson were atheists, he is either ignorant of US history, or he is lying. Washington and Jefferson were both confirmed Freemasons. Freemasonry is very much a religion, a religion that includes one called god. With promises of power and wealth, the Freemason organization will accept any denominational background into its membership, just so long as the recruit is willing to swear a blood oath to secrecy. After many years in Freemasonry, the member may rise to a high enough level to learn the *"secrets of the craft"*. If you should reach the 30th degree in Freemasonry, certain *"secret knowledge"* or *"ancient wisdom"* will be revealed to you, and that information is that Lucifer is in fact god, and now you can tap his energies. That's what the big secret is. Most Freemasons are clueless as to where the ship that they have boarded is taking them, they actually believe that they are in some kind of harmless, charitable, fraternal order.

Some Christian historians rationalize that Freemasonry must have been compatible with Christianity in colonial times. Not the case, it was a blood oath secret society with Satan as the cherry on top then, and the same is true now. One possibility is that any Christians who could have found the two religions compatible would have been ignorant of what is at the heart of Freemasonry. Perhaps the colonial Christians had been deceived. I mean like at least 42% of today's evangelicals voted for an infanticide legislating, Christ mocking Barack Obama to be their president, think about it. At least 60% of evangelicals believe that there are multiple paths to heaven, just different faiths leading to the same heaven. This is haunting evidence for me that the majority of people that call themselves Christians do not grasp the most basic fundamentals regarding eternal life. The other possibility of how a Christian nation could have an Illuminati inspired government is that the only way that a politician could get elected in a Christian society was to pretend to be a Christian, deception is common practice in Freemasonry. I voted for George W. Bush, believing his professions of faith in Christ, unaware of his affiliation and loyalty to the Skull and Bones secret society, the aristocratic ranks of Freemasonry. Based upon legislation records of the presidential candidates, I would have still voted for "W" as the less dangerous of the two. John Kerry was in the same secret society. I would love to recant my statements about "W", but first "W" would have to denounce the Skull and Bones. "W" would also have to admit that there are not *"many paths to the Almighty"*. That would make his status of born again brother seem a lot more legitimate in my eyes. Many US presidents have been in secret occult societies that are branches of the Illuminati. The non-partisan goal is the forming of the New World Order. One of the last things that JFK ever did was threaten to expose a secret society that was covertly running the US government, it's pretty easy to find and listen to JFK's speech online.

"The real rulers in Washington are invisible and exercise power from behind the scenes." Felix Frankfurtern (US Supreme Court Justice, who died in 1965.)

Whether we like it or not, the formation of the US government was greatly influenced by Freemasons using the blood and treasure of hard working, professing Christians that were seeking religious freedom and tax relief. Christians greatly influenced American policy, this is clear history. It is true that this influence has been diminished to the point that it is now almost nonexistent. This is the effect that Lyell / Darwinian "science" has on a nation when it is pedaled to young minds as if it were fact. In this type of world view, enslaving dark skinned, less evolved animals seem acceptable. Eventually killing unborn and newborn babies with tax dollars becomes the norm. Over 25% of African American children will be killed by a human butcher either before birth or shortly after they are born. Now that's Darwinian progress. Where would science be without this great theory?

This may be news to Dawkins, but almost all US citizens at her beginning were professing Christians seeking freedom to worship, however, the original US government was formed out of the Freemason ideology more so than Christianity. Some estimates have at up to 50 of the 56 signatures on the Declaration of Independence being the signatures of men that were known to be Freemasons. Although god is referenced, Christ Jesus is never mentioned. Who was the god that they were referencing and trusting? Freemasons were responsible for unionizing the original colonies and also for instigating the Boston tea party in an effort to get a full blown revolution under way. Many historians know that the Freemasons were instrumental in stirring up the revolution that would ultimately bring about US sovereignty.

Please take notice that 106 of the first 108 colleges in the United States were Christian, yes Christian; this should be a powerful indicator as to the ideology of the vast majority of the US citizens at her beginning. Read their textbooks and their declarations of Christ being the foundation of all sound learning. How could Dawkins be this ignorant? He just couldn't be, perhaps he has ambitions to rewrite history the way he wished it had gone down. The United States was a Christian society from her very beginning with a government that had a hidden Freemasonic occult agenda. Washington DC was designed by Freemasons. Everything from the layout of the city streets forming a pentagram, to the city's location on the 77th meridian were done in accordance with Freemasonic design.

If you ever take a tour of Washington DC, you will quickly discover that the city is just covered with the Illuminati's Masonic/ Luciferic symbolism, while evidence for Christianity is absent. For an in depth probe into the inner workings of the Illuminati, the hierarchy of

Freemasonry and all the other Satanic secret societies, I would encourage you to listen to what John Todd has to say about this subject. John Todd was a former Satanist member of the Illuminati, he would eventually denounce the occult and expose the secrets of the Illuminati. His story is riveting, with insights that could only come from an insider. John Todd was drugged, jailed, and has disappeared, and no one seems to know for sure what happened to him. You can hear hear John Todd's audio testimonies by searching Youtube.com for **"John Todd Explains The Illuminati"**. The audio information will really awaken you to the inner workings of this occult scheme for the New World Order, which has been millennia in the making.

Dawkins never mentions the influence that Freemasonry had in the US government since the nation's beginning. Why not? Either Dawkins is ignorant or he lying about it. This is a very strange way to attempt to prove evolution. Why would Dawkins even chase this founding fathers rabbit leading to nowhere? This is just so bizarre, especially when you consider the fact that atheism had zero influence on the original colonies and the founding government of the United States. I suppose that Dawkins could have just been creating fluff for his non-scientific book, for the purpose of making money by selling books to people who want to comfortably live a lifestyle that is opposed to God's plan for their life.

For fun, let's suppose that every single US citizen, congressmen and president has been atheist since day one. That would prove that the universe created itself from a spinning dot? That would prove that mankind spontaneously generated out of mud soup? It really does not matter what great names Dawkins attempts to tie to evolutionism, his religion is dumb and dangerous... Gee, if a man as great as Thomas Jefferson was an atheist, uh, then I should be one too, duh.

Are Dawkins readers really that gullible? Or do they just desperately want to believe that they are in the company of great minds? Thomas Jefferson and George Washington were not atheists, they were Freemasons.

I expect that some people reading this will refuse to believe that the United States had Freemasonic origins, and that many of our founding fathers were anything less than Bible beating saints. Feel free not to trust what I am telling you, do your own research. I did not believe many things the first time I learned them, because I had to let go of cherished beliefs. But when examining evidence from a non bias approach, I had to accept a new reality.

Several years ago, I believed that president "W" was sincere and that his motives were pure... I was duped. His professions of faith and biblical references do not measure up with the direction that "W" took the United States. Back then, I saw "W" as a Christian who was bringing liberation and religious freedom to the Muslim world. Today I view "W" as having taken orders from the Illuminati to advance their New World Order agenda. "W" delivered on some of his token promises to the conservative right, while at the same time he steered our nation toward a North American Union with Canada and Mexico, that will soon be established and enforced, probably in my lifetime, certainly in the life of my children. This NAU will be one of 10 unions that will cover the entire planet and will be governed by the New World Order.

I believe that this approach that "W" took, that got him into office, by saying one thing but intending something quite different, is the same approach that the founding fathers took when establishing this nation. They had to make our founding documents palatable to Bible believing voters or they would not have been empowered to orchestrate their scheme. Take a close look at DC and tell me that this city was designed and decked by Jesus loving Christians. I hated to let go of some cherished beliefs, but when faced with the evidence, I simply had to. Some people refuse to let go of their cherished beliefs for very noble reasons. Some reason that if they could just prove that our founding fathers were devout, sincere Christians, then that will give them the upper hand in the confrontation against the socialist left and their anti-God agenda, and against the Marxist judges that legislate from the bench. Although their intentions are noble, the only thing that is ever going to reverse the direction of this economically and morally bankrupt nation, is if all true believers will stop playing games and humble themselves and pray.

If this information is painfully contrary to all you thought you knew about US history, then I am sorry. As I demonstrated in the previous chapter, textbooks are not committed to the truth. Textbooks are designed to persuade minds to believe what the government wants them to believe. Don't slay the messenger for being committed to the truth.

The high ranking Freemasons may be diluted enough to believe that Lucifer is really god, but they are not so pathetic that they cannot see the creation as evidence of a Creator. I do not believe that Dawkins is that pathetic either. Perhaps it is time for Dawkins to come clean. I am forced to consider the possibility that Dawkins is deliberately working against a God that he knows exists. I believe that the mission for Dawkins is dethroning a Creator that deep down he knows is real, while generating as much revenue as he possibly can. I do not believe that Dawkins is an atheist. Dawkins should be honest and liberate himself. Look, I do not want to judge or condemn Dawkins; I do not have the authority to do so. I am simply trying to remove the cloak of deception that Dawkins seems to have wrapped himself in. The reason that I took the time and effort to expose the US government's Illuminati, Freemasonic origins was not done just to expose Dawkins' ignorance of US history. The reason that I elaborated in such detail on the topic will make a lot more sense in the latter chapters of this book, as we expose evolutionism's hidden agenda.

A not so Great Prayer Experiment

So Dawkins prints this "scientific study" that proves that prayer does not work. It's such a bogus sham, it's laughable. Would you believe that Dawkins, a "scientist", would ascribe to the belief that if there were a God then the royal family in England should be the most healthy, because the whole country is praying for them? Prayers said out of obligation or to curry favor from those who govern your nation would hardly constitute communication with God. If Dawkins were a scientist, he would wonder how it is that a family that practices inbreeding would be as healthy as the rest of the population. The whole report is just silly, I have no idea how even an atheist could not see the flaws in it. It is poorly documented propaganda that was obviously trumped up to refute all of the legitimate studies showing the effectiveness of prayer.

Prayer is a force, a force that can have beneficial effects for even atheists, if the one saying the prayer sincerely believes. I do not need to ponder why the details surrounding the "study" were so vague. Let's have some details sir. The study was not scientific and flawed on so many levels. I mean just google "prayer promotes healing survey" and look at the results. I saw the results from several studies and the percentage of American doctors that attest to prayer promoting healing ranged from 80% to 99% depending on the survey. The testimonies from patients and doctors about miracle healing from prayer and faith go on and on and on. I was unable to find any testimonies that a disease or cancer just magically went away and nobody was praying for a miracle. Evolutionism prophets have lied to us about radio-metric dating, a geologic column, the age of the earth, and the Pangea fantasy, so it should be no surprise that Dawkins would mislead us about the results of prayer to muster up a shred of credibility for his religion. It was really refreshing for me to learn that so many American physicians still revere the power of prayer. Now, let's look at some statistics that Dawkins attempted to wish away with his bias "scientific study"...

"The federal government has spent $ 2.2 million in the past five years on studies of distant healing, which have drawn support from private foundations.

San Francisco Cardiologist Randolph Byrd, for example, conducted an experiment in which he asked born again Christians to pray for 192 people hospitalized with heart problems, comparing them with 201 not targeted for prayer. No one knew which group they were in. He reported in 1988 that those who were prayed for needed fewer drugs and less help breathing.

William S. Harris of St. Luke Hospital in Kansas City Mo., and colleagues published similar results in 1999 from a study involving nearly 1,000 heart patients, about half of whom were prayed for without their knowledge."

Rob Stein
Washington Post
March 24th, 2006

Keep in mind that the Washington Post is not a Christian newspaper, here we have an unbiased journalist reporting his findings. This just scratches the surface. Do your own research and you will find overwhelming evidence that Christian prayer is a powerful influence in the healing process. God can heal. God can give grace to endure. God can take someone into eternity. He is God, and He has an incomprehensible, sovereign will. It seems that Dawkins has confused God with the imaginary Genie in a bottle. God is far too infinite to ever be put into any of man's little boxes. If Dawkins has no reverence for God's sovereign will, this would in no way obligate God to conform to the wishes of, or the experiments of men. Denial of a Creator, in spite of the overwhelming evidence in the creation, in no way excludes one from certain judgment by that Creator.

Chapter Four

Why There Most Certainly is a God

Who Dunnit?

The following is a verbatim quote from Richard Dawkins during his interview with Ben Stein. Stein included this clip in the movie *Expelled, No Intelligence Allowed*. The movie documentary is very interesting and never boring as it brings to light the oppressive injustice inflicted upon college professors and researchers who have had the audacity to trust the evidence for creation. The movie also illuminates the genocidal results of evolutionism. *Expelled* is a very informative movie documentary that I highly recommend. This is the quote by Dawkins;

"It could be that at some earlier time somewhere in the universe a civilization evolved by probably some kind of Darwinian means to a very, very high level of technology and designed the form of life that they seated on to. That is a possibility, an intriguing possibility and I suppose it's possible that you might find evidence of that if you look at the details of biochemistry and molecular biology, you

might find some sort of designer, and the designer could well be a higher intelligence from elsewhere in the universe." - Richard Dawkins

Okay, here we have Mr. Dawkins conveniently tiptoeing away from the fundamental teaching of the religion of evolutionism. Is this the same man who said *"We can now safely say that the illusion of design in living creatures is just that - an illusion."* ? Now Dawkins concedes that perhaps intelligent design is no longer an illusion, but since he is so bent on denying the existence of God, then ET must have done it. Since the "illusion of design" was really his delusion, then perhaps the illusion of ET is really just more of the same - his delusion. If someone can be gullible enough to spend decades promoting the idea that a speck of dust created all the energy, time and space in the cosmos, then it should not surprise us that their journey to reality may includes pit stops in science fiction. Keep in mind that this is the person who says *"The scientific enterprise is an active seeking, an active seeking out of gaps in our knowledge, seeking out of ignorance so that we can work to plug that ignorance."* - RD. When Richard Dawkins finally comes to the realization that intelligent design is not only likely, but provable, he quickly abandons the notion that dirt soup turned into every plant and animal, and concedes, well, aliens may have done it. Aliens did it? Is that plugging our ignorance, Richard? Thanks for plugging our ignorance, Richard. Where would science be without these great contributions? What really boggles the mind is that Dawkins even has his cult following. I hope they are not waiting for some comet to whisk them into Shangrila. This is the kind of thoughtless, blind devotion to a cult that can lead to CNN footage of a mansion full of dead, kool-aid people wearing Nike's and purple shrouds. It's very alarming when people blindly devote themselves to a cult leader without giving one thought to reason or reality.

"Everyone of these difficult questions that comes up, science says right, let's roll up our sleeves and work on it. Religion says oh, God did it." -RD. So here we have a clear example of the die hard dedication Dawkins has to his religion. Instead of saying oh, God did it, Dawkins has resorted to saying, oh, aliens did it. Evolutionism is without a doubt the most fantastic of all the organized religions. You see, Dawkins himself is not even convinced that life on earth is a result of naturalistic processes that took billions of years. He is just pedaling a religion for profit. Is Dawkins really any different than any of those crooked religious gurus that hustle devotees out of their money? Dawkins will say just about anything that he deems necessary to expand disbelief for a Creator and pedal his books. When Dawkins cannot deny the signature of a Creator, that's right ladies and gentlemen, then aliens did it. Where would science be without this great contribution?

I suspect at some point in the future, when the memory of Richard Dawkins is fading, Dawkins will come forward with a report that he has actually met a little green alien that informed him that we were in fact planted here by aliens that evolved long ago and far way from a bacteria in another distant galaxy (by Darwinian means, of course). The reason I strongly suspect Dawkins will go this route is because when people are this devoted to a religion, for example the Nazis under Hitler, or the cultists under Jim Jones, they tend to let go of reality. The blind faithful tend to trade their ability to rationally compute, in exchange for a brainwashed allegiance to their cult, rejecting reality and clinging to fantasy in an attempt to calm the confusion that is erupting within.

As the scientific evidence continues to mount, destroying notions that the universe might have created itself, and obliterating the possibility of spontaneous generation of life, you will see this alien creator theory snowball. As the holes in the theory of evolution become so clear, the more far out you will see the creation rejecter reach to find a solution to the dilemma. It's already happening, the aliens visiting and enlightening humanity propaganda is being turned on full blast by the media. Hollywood is turning out movies on a regular basis that show aliens as super intelligent, high tech life forms (both friends and foes), that could really enlighten us, or possibly threaten us. The Illuminati propagandists want the public to believe that we have elite super stealthy aliens infiltrating our society and our governments. This is Illuminati propaganda. Any "visitations" and "enlightenment" that is going on is called demonic interaction. There are in fact secret forces at work in society and government, but they are not visitors from Super Mario Galaxy, they are spirits of demons visiting our dimension.

For they are spirits of demons, performing signs, which go out to the kings of the earth and of the whole world, to gather them to the battle of that great day of God Almighty. Revelation 16:14 NKJV

Make no mistake, the god of evolutionism is pure evil, and as the lies unravel, new fantastic propaganda is fabricated. You must willingly believe lies and convince yourself of fictional fantasies to make the religion of evolutionism palatable.

Sticks and Stones

"It is absolutely safe to say that if you meet someone who claims not to believe in evolution, that person is ignorant, stupid or insane."
Richard Dawkins, *Put Your Money on Evolution, NY Times*; April 9th, 1999

If one's world view is such that anyone who does not agree with them is ignorant, stupid or insane, this should be a good indicator that the person is bound by an unhealthy devotion to a cult style of faith. Here Dawkins demonstrates his hostility toward anyone that does not bow down to the golden ape of evolutionism. Calling me ignorant would be understandable to me, knowing that we are all ignorant about far more than we are knowledgeable about. Calling me ignorant about the origins of the universe and the origins of life would be a lot more specific, and it would also be understandable coming from someone that has been successfully indoctrinated into the religion of evolutionism. What I do not understand however, is why Dawkins would assert that a person's belief in a Creator constitutes their stupidity or insanity. This is the precise kind of intolerant hatred that drives the "higher evolved" mad men to unleash their brutality on humanity. I will not go as far as to call Dawkins stupid or insane, although it is very clear that his world view has had a very stupid and insane impact on humanity. I will be so bold as to call Dawkins religiously indoctrinated, that's right, brainwashed into a belief system that is not only unproven but very disprovable.

Does Mr. Dawkins really know everything? When you consider all of the information out there, I mean just consider that one person's DNA, if decoded, that one person's DNA contains enough information to write enough books to fill every dump truck in the world with fine print. A person could not even live long enough to read their own DNA code. It is safe to say that Mr. Dawkins does not even know 1% of all there is to know. To make this point, let's pretend that Dawkins knows half of all there is to know. How can Dawkins be certain that God does not exist within the half that he does not know? How can Dawkins judge people on an issue that he is totally ignorant of? If Charles Darwin had even an inkling of how complex one DNA molecule was, he would likely not have concocted evolutionism. We know that the religion of evolutionism has indeed been concocted, and when things like DNA show the impossibility random chance, instead of letting go of the diehard dedication to the religion, new fantasies are concocted, and aliens are welcomed into the formation process. In recent years it has finally dawned on Dawkins that you cannot fill trillions of books with information without an Author. There must be an Author of life. So I believe *"In the beginning God"*, and Dawkins believes *"In the beginning alien wizards"*. How does that make me stupid and Dawkins smart? How does that make me insane and Dawkins sane?

Even the DNA molecule for the single celled bacterium, E.coli, contains enough information to fill all of the books in any of the world's largest libraries.
allaboutscience.org/dna-double-helix.htm

A renowned mathematician and astronomer by the name of Sir Frederick Hoyle once calculated the possibility of the formation of just one simple enzyme forming by chance is 1 in 10 to the power of 20 (1 in 100,000,000,000,000,000,000). Now, that is just one simple enzyme, nowhere near what is needed for a single protein. It would take roughly 2,000 of these enzymes to entertain the possibility of a cell, they would need to form by atoms just moving about randomly.

The odds of this impossibility are 1 in 10 to the 40,000th power. That number is greater than the number of atoms in the universe. I could peck out that long number and create huge chapters of fluff, but unlike Mr. Dawkins, I am not that desperate for fluff. I prefer to deal in facts not fluff, besides, acres of forest would need to be turned into paper in order to put that number into print. Please consider that all of the atoms in the universe are numbered at roughly 10 to the 80th power. Even atheist critics have had to concede that Hoyle's mathematical computations are fairly accurate. I am a former gambling man and I wouldn't bet one cent with a million dollar pay off on those odds. It just does not happen.

For fun, let's suppose it did happen, an asexual self repli-cating cell actually some how evolved into a sexually repro-ductive living organism. What are the odds of another living organism of the opposite sex, suitable for mating, popping out in the same place throughout all of time and space? I don't know, I am not a mathematician, but I am certain that the odds would be one in a number that would wrap around the universe an infinite number of times. To believe in such fantastic and impossible odds could be viewed as stupid or insane I suppose, but I will refrain from reciprocating the name calling. The sheer mathematical impossibility would force any logical gambling man to totally reject the possi-bility of life spontaneously generating out of mud soup. I am shocked that Dawkins has the audacity to call his beliefs science and belief in a Creator stupid or insane.

No honest scientific mind would promote mathematical impossibilities as possible. Don't tell me that Dawkins' faith is not religious and mine is, not the case, they are both reli-gious. Dawkins' faith is way more religious than mine is. Evolutionism requires greater faith in mathematical impos-sibilities than anything I believe. These mathematical computations also rule out the chance of alien life forms evolving long ago and far away by Darwinian means. I will not go out of my way to offend Mr. Dawkins but nor shall I don kid gloves when addressing the sheer absurdity in placing blind religious faith in mathematical impossibilities. It is safe to say that if you meet someone that has placed their money on evolutionism, that person has little concept of mathematical probability and that person has placed a losing bet. A much safer bet would be to bet that you will win the power ball lottery the next 1,000 times in row. It just doesn't happen. Reflect on Dawkins guess that a Creator is 99% improbable (*"indeed"*), and then please consider this... If Dawkins had been weighing science and mathematical computations, instead of making his wild guesses, he most certainly would have drawn a very different conclusion.

Life's Fundamental Questions

There are four fundamental questions in life, that humans have this unexplainable need to find answers to, and every single religion, including evolutionism, tries to come up with the answers to these four questions. To address these questions I would like to pose these questions and give you the answers according to the religion of evolutionism;

1. Origin: Where did I come from?

Evolutionism's answer - You are not God's creation. You are a product of random chance; a bacteria that crawled out of a mud pit. You share a common heritage with cockroaches.

2. Meaning: What is the meaning to life?

Evolutionism's answer - There is no meaning. Live for this moment. The fittest survive, the weak die. There is no soul, a person's worth consists of the substances that they are composed of.

3. Morality: Who defines right and wrong?

Evolutionism's answer - No one defines right and wrong, so do whatever seems right to you. There is no consequence to behavior. Enjoy your time here because that's all you have.

4. Destiny: Where will I go when I die?

Evolutionism's answer - There is no after life, you simply decompose and your body will be recycled as a daisy or a dung beetle.

This is what has been taught in public schools for the past 5 decades. This leaves the student with no God to take refuge in during times of trouble, and no hope for their eternity. It is no wonder we have seen spikes in all the areas of morality in this time period. STD's, drug use, and violent crimes have all sky rocketed since the infiltration of evolutionism into academics. We now have new types of music in our society, like Satanic heavy metal, and hypnotic sounds and destructive lyrics to suit just about every type of musical preference. This warp in thinking would also usher in new laws that would make sacrificing unborn and newborn children legal and tax funded. What should we expect when we tell kids that they are animals without a God, that there is no moral law and no consequence to animalistic behavior? Garbage in, garbage out. The evolutionism ideology promotes "racism" (shadism), cultural intolerance, socialism, communism, humanism, genocide, eugenics, abortion and euthanasia. All of these isms lead to the same end, that end is one human's elevation through the death and oppression of other humans, and why not? Humans are the problem, the more of these carbon emitting, cancerous, earth destroyers that we can exterminate, the better off mother earth would be and the more rapidly those of us in the more *"highly evolved gene pool"* could advance onward toward god-like status. **FYI** - The reason you always see the word "racism" written as a quote, is because I believe that it is an invalid label for defining the variations within humankind. Humans are born with different colors, but we are all human and all of the same race. If the mother rabbit gives birth to a black, a brown and a white bunny all in the same litter, does that mean that they are a different species because they are different colors? Of course not, that's ridiculous. "Races" within humanity was just concocted by some evolutionary mind, that no doubt deemed himself of the more highly evolved gene pool. Being one human species, it would be accurate to call intolerance based upon one's shade or skin color, shadism. The only reason that I write "racism" is so the reader will know what I am talking about. Perhaps the next dictionary published by good old Webster will include my new word, shadism. Pardon me for my compulsion to chase that "racist" rabbit.

Let me return to the point that I was making. Please ponder the genius clarity in the response that Dr. Ravi Zacharias gives to these four basic questions.

1. Non Physical
No physical entity or quantity does not have the reason for existence in itself. Ultimately the physical universe reduced in any form cannot explain its own origin. It has to find an explanation outside of itself. It has to have something non physical as its cause. -Dr. Ravi Zacharias

2. Intellectual
Not from design but to design. If you walk onto a planet and see a wrapper from a McDonalds hamburger and see letters of an alphabet, you immediately know that there is information there, and logic tells you, as it tells everyone listening, where you see information you assume that prior to that information is a mind. You don't think that the dictionary developed because of an explosion at a printing press. There is sequence to the whole thing. -Dr. Ravi Zacharias

3. History
The moral issues, social issues and just human intercourse demands the explanation of a moral reality. So if you've got a first cause that is spiritual, a first cause that is mind, a first cause that needs to explain morality, you take these three struggles. Pause with me for a moment. There are four fundamental questions in life; origin, meaning, morality, and destiny. You take these four questions and these three explanations needed and only God is big enough to explain this universe. -Dr. Ravi Zacharias

Richard Dawkins believes that cosmic evolution is *"just waiting for its Darwin"*. Well, that's going to require the emergence of another genocide advocating, "racist", sexist like Darwin, capable of convincing people that a speck of dust exploded into the infinite number of stars, and the foam of galaxies. There is no evolutionary answer for the origin of time, space and matter. This should sway a thinking mind to consider the possibility of a Creator.

I would like to purpose those same four fundamental life questions again without denying the clear, rational, over-whelming evidence that indicates that there is undoubtedly a Creator of time, space and matter.

1. Origin: Where did I come from?

My answer - I came from an all powerful divine Creator, Who loves me enough to create me in His own image. I am special to God, so special in fact, that God believes that I am worth dying for.

2. Meaning: What is the meaning to life?

My answer - God has a plan and a purpose for our lives. We are meant to have a loving relationship with the Creator, serving Him by declaring His love and by serving the needs of humanity.

3. Morality: Who defines right from wrong?

My answer - God's moral laws define right from wrong. God's plan for us is to do His will and adhere to His pre-cepts, for our own well being as much as others. We must love others as we love ourselves. This is the only moral com-pass that could successfully navigate human society.

4. Destiny: Where will I go when I die?

My answer - To spend eternity with the Creator, because I have received the Gift of eternal life through a relationship with the Son of God, Christ Jesus, Yeshua the Messiah.

When we contrast the ideologies of creation and evolutionism, it is easy to see why the religion of evolutionism has caused so much death and destruction. No respect for human life, no moral consequence or accountability. Nothing is sacred. Children growing up being taught evolutionism have no God to turn to and no eternity in which they can place any hope in. Without a God to be accountable to, and without an eternity to consider, men are left entirely to their own whims and reasoning. Without God, atheistic men have been able to scheme up the only possible result in the absence of their Creator. Atheists have produced for this world a religion of misery and death.

Reasoning Evil

Because no evidence exists for evolution, and there is overwhelming evidence of a Creator, people committed to denying a Creator often grasp at straws, reasoning, *"If there is a God, then why does so much evil go on in this world?"*. There is one thing that we can all agree on, and this is that there certainly is a lot of evil in this world. The fact that there is evil in the world in no way disproves God's goodness. Evil in the world only proves man's wickedness and man's need for a good and righteous Savior. In any field of academic study we see that factors always have opposites. We have numbers like +100 and -100 (opposites), we have hot and cold, light and dark, wet and dry, or introvert and extrovert. The opposition is simply present, that's just the way it is. The fact that there is such low down, dark, evil, cowardly hatred is clear evidence that there is a high, brilliant, loving, holy God. How can any atheist rationally reason that there just cannot be a God because of all of the evil in the world?

This atheistic notion just begs the following questions that I would challenge any atheist to rationally answer; Mr.

atheist, is there even such a thing as evil in this Godless world? When the atheist considers the atrocities unleashed on humanity by evil men, they will have to confess, yes, there is evil in the world. Well, then there must be good, the opposite of evil, right? Is there good? Again the cornered atheist will have to concede and answer yes. Then Mr. atheist, should we have scales or some kind of laws differentiating good or acceptable behavior from evil or unacceptable behavior? The cornered atheist will respond, yes. Then we need a law giver, right? The cornered atheist will answer, yes, I guess we do. But Mr. atheist you have already denied a law giver so evil does not even exist in your mind. Allegiance to the faith of evolutionism cripples one's ability to rationally compute. How can a mind with no absolutes be so absolutely sure there is no God?

If one refuses to believe in the goodness of God due to lack of evidence, how could one deny the presence of demonic evil, based on the evidence? We can't have darkness without light. We cannot have evil without good. They are simply polar opposites. The evidence of one is clear evidence of the other. You cannot deny a Creator based on anything less than wishful thinking, denial, or a blind hatred toward an authority figure called God. There is just no scientific rationale for such a world view. When you hear an atheist like Dawkins get worked up and start ranting his utter contempt for God, one has to give pause and wonder... Why would some fictional character like God, as fictional as Mickey Mouse, generate so much hatred in a professing atheist like Dawkins? It does not take a PhD in psychology to conclude that deep in his heart, Dawkins believes that God is real, and that one day God will judge him.

I hope it's becoming clear how much confusion the atheist must accept to maintain their world view. In defiance of all reasoning, atheists enjoy the creation without a Creator. Atheists enjoy design at every level, from molecular to galactic, without a Designer. Atheists claim moral law is warranted, but without a moral law giver. I do not believe for a moment that any atheist or agnostic is really without a god. Everyone has a god of some kind, perhaps self, materialism, whatever, but all false gods lead in the same direction, away from the one true living God, and toward the god of death and destruction. I do not want to sound judgmental, but I do want to express my sincere concern by sounding the alarm and waking up the atheist to the reality that they are already on the course of eternity, and that the fork in the road is straightaway.

Reasoning Suffering

Suffering proves there is no God. Since scientific evidence cannot prove there is no God, perhaps the fact that people suffer means there is no God. Atheists like to reason that there just cannot be a God because of all of the suffering in the world. Suffering is bad, no doubt about it, but unlike an atheist, I can view suffering from an eternal perspective. We are on this earth but a moment, however, eternity is forever. Please consider my brief analogies. Have you ever met someone in peak athletic condition? They are strong, lean, long winded and confident. Can you imagine this person, feeling the high that comes from being in peak athletic condition, telling you this? "It just wasn't worth it, all that blood, sweat and tears, and all I have to show for it is this strong, healthy body and extreme confidence, I wish I could undo the pain, and be fat and lethargic." No, you can't imagine that. The suffering had a payoff. Likewise, I am reasonably certain that no rational woman giving birth to a child enjoys the pain and suffering associated with birthing a child. When that child is born, the pain and suffering are so miniscule in comparison with the reward. After the birth of my three children, on every occasion, the joy from holding the new child pushed all my wife's memories of the pain completely out of her consciousness. A few hours of painful labor, followed by decades of joy and parental fulfillment, a loving relationship that both persons believe can never be broken. The love between a mother and her child is indescribable. How much greater is the love of the heavenly Father? God's original plan did not include suffering, man brought that upon himself by deliberately deviating from God's plan for his life by disobeying. It was man's sin that brought suffering into the world, not God. God can however, allow suffering to serve as beneficial.

When I was a person who refused to believe in God, I couldn't help but notice that when I was successful I partied and when I was a failure, I found time to ponder. My failures brought me much pain and suffering, but the pondering that went along with that suffering would eventually illuminate my need for a Savior. It's easy for me to see how God can use suffering to promote the pondering that might cause one to consider God. I will not lie and say that believing God's promises and accepting His Gift has made my life free from suffering, in many respects life has become much more difficult. When I was a party hound, I seemed to be cool enough, an alright guy, accepted by almost everyone I met. When I made an effort to serve God and reach out to the poor in the neediest parts of the world, this is when vicious and oppressive attacks against me and my family began, these attacks continue to this day. Don't be naive enough to believe that if you accept your Creator as your Lord and Savior that it will bring an end to all of your pain and suffering. The Lord can give you peace in spite of your pain and suffering, but He never promised to alleviate all suffering in this life here on this present earth. As sure as suffering drew me to God, perhaps out of desperation, it would not be long before more suffering would draw me into an even deeper relationship with God, out of adoration as opposed to desperation. Step by step God can use your suffering to conform you into a greater likeness of His Son. This is His desire for all of us, even for Mr. Dawkins, that none of us should perish but that all of us would come to repentance, and be conformed to the image of Christ Jesus, Yeshua. Suffering can actually serve as a refining process. To say that there cannot be a God because there is suffering is to not have considered God's infinite wisdom in which we cannot begin to comprehend. I think it is interesting that the believers in the third world, who have seen loved ones starved to death and even murdered, are the sincerest believers, this is an example of suffering producing faith as solid as a stone. These people do not ponder the status of their retirement plan, nor do they spend a whole lot of time day dreaming about their next vacation or get away. Their eyes are fixed on the real prize. They have nothing but the blessed hope, and for a true believer, that's enough.

Unbelievers Suffer

For the unbeliever, suffering may give one reason to ponder the possibility of a loving God that could grant them peace and the assurance of eternal life in the midst of their trials. When the Lord allows your life to be shaken up, it's for a purpose, to break that false sense of security that so many unbelievers put their trust in. Busted retirement plans, property values spiraling down, or perhaps being incarcerated or perhaps a major illness, or the illness or loss of a loved one. The list goes on of the things in life that can cause human suffering. Suffering gives opportunity for the unbeliever to seek security outside of themselves and reach for divine security. When one's pride is inflated to a certain point, calamity has a way of bursting that bubble, producing a humbled heart, softening a person's heart so that it might be penetrated by true security. Unfortunately, many unbelievers feel that their calamity is a cause to be bitter or angry, this is when it seems like suffering is wasted. Suffering can be a call to seek the Lord ...

And Jesus answered and said to them, "Do you suppose that these Galileans were worse sinners than all the other Galileans, because they suffered such things? " I tell you no; but unless you repent you will all likewise perish. "Or those eighteen on whom the tower of Siloam fell and killed them, do you think that they were worse sinners than all the other men who dwelt in Jerusalem? " I tell you, no; but unless you repent you will all likewise perish."
Luke 13:2-5 NKJV

I am a sinner, I am just as guilty as any atheist, however, I have received a pardon, not based on my righteousness or any righteousness that I might some day muster. My pardon is based entirely on the goodness of God, Christ paying the price for my sins. His righteousness will be credited to me on judgment day, not because I am good, but because God is so good.

Believers Suffer

For the believing Christian, suffering provides opportunities for spiritual growth. Perseverance over suffering in the life of a believer can provide unbelievers with a demonstration of peace or joy that can be found in spite of the circumstances when one's faith and hope are on eternity. Suffering can strengthen us to share our belief in God. Suffering can test our faith. Faith being tested by suffering can lead to spiritual maturity to handle the responsibility of God's purpose for your life on earth, as well as your eternal life. Suffering can be like the refining of gold in the life of a believer, extraction of impurities, increasing purity. The true believers may have their faith shaken to it's very foundation by traumatic events, but the believer has the blessed faith that all problems are momentary and eternity with God is forever. I want to emphasize that no suffering in the life of a believer is wasted, the suffering is not in vain. It will be used by God to fashion the character of His child.

And not only that, but we also glorify in tribulations, knowing that tribulation produces perseverance: and perseverance, character: and character, hope.
Romans 5: 3, 4 NKJV

And He said to me, "My grace is sufficient for you, for My strength is made perfect in weakness." Therefore most gladly will I rather boast in my infirmities, that the power of Christ may rest upon me.
II Corinthians 12:9 NKJV

In spite of all the evil that this world will hurl at believers, believers hold on to the blessed hope, believing His promises in spite of the most intense suffering. It is my hope that this section will help someone else as much as it helped me, I really needed to hear it. For some people, like me, lessons just cannot be learned well, until we teach them. I wasted so many years counting tribulations and personal attacks as something that could impact my peace of mind. If I had been resting on these scriptures, I could have spared myself a great deal of heartache and pain. Loving and praying for your enemies is easy to say, but it is so difficult to do (for me anyway), but if I had known the peace and relief that accompanies this practice, then I would have aggressively pursued it years ago. I have come to believe that God wants us to love and pray for our enemies for our own sake as much as for the sake of the enemy. Holding on to anger and bitterness, wishing evil on someone, or pondering paybacks is a kin to drinking poison with the hope that it will make your enemy suffer.

For I reckon that the sufferings of this present time are not worthy to be compared with the glory which shall be revealed in us.
Romans 8:18 KJV

Chapter Five

A Closer Look at Religion

Religion vs. Truth

"Moths fly into a candle flame, and it doesn't look like an accident. We could label it ' self - immolation behavior ' and, under that provocative name, wonder how on earth natural selection could favour it." Richard Dawkins, *The God Delusion*

Moths fly into flames, and there you have it ladies and gentlemen, proof that the universe created itself from a spinning dot 20 billion years ago, and that 4 billion years ago a bacteria in your family tree created itself from mud, or did really smart alien wizards place the moths and the humans, which they invented, here on this planet that they created... I just can't decide, but it sure as heck wasn't God! I must admit that I can relate to Dawkins' analogy regarding so many of religion's devotees being equated to moths drawn to flames. Without the truth, even the extremely religious person is still destined for a miserable eternity, but not because of any "misfire" in some "natural selection" process.

What's interesting is that the moths like religious people have fairly clean hands when they are compared to the blood soaked hands of the atheist mad men that have herded hundreds of millions of humans into the slaughter. We know that the words religion and truth have very different definitions. Many people have died in vain as a result of their devotion to their religion but no one has ever died in vain for the truth. Many have murdered innocent people for the advancement of their religion (the evolutionism religion being the greatest culprit), but no one has ever murdered for the advancement of the truth. Religion can require many hoops for one to jump through, but truth is without hoops. Religion is merely a temporary fix at best, but truth is everlasting.

Understand that a person devoted to truth can be fairly labeled religious but I am going to be so bold as to hypothesize that at least 95% of religious behavior is void of truth, or is perhaps a mixture of lies and truth. A mixture of lies and truth is no longer truth. One quart of milk with just a few drops of poison added is no longer milk, it is now poisoned milk and unfit for consumption. All the religious fervor one can muster will never bridge the gap between that person and God, only truth can bridge that gap. When people render religious loyalty to an institution void of core truth, they will subject themselves to the ever changing whims of men, this often leaves the devotee trusting in the reasoning of control freaks, perverts, greedy con men, power trippers, god wannabe's, and even genocidal mass murderers in some cases. Religion has been and still is used to achieve monetary gain or to advance a military or political agenda. I don't think this is a secret to anyone.

It seems that mankind has always held the notion that life must be about embracing a cause bigger than one's self, even when it means going to war or dying for their beliefs.

Empowered mad men have often been able to capitalize on people's religious loyalty to god and country. This inherent psychology of man's will to be part of something bigger than himself, loyal to a greater cause for a greater good, simply does not fit into the evolutionary psychology scheme, which insists that man is really just an animal whose mind is "set up" by a process of "natural selection" for the pursuit of self preservation. This rather points to the contrary; this is evidence that man was created with this unexplainable desire to find a greater meaning to life than being fit enough to survive. People are always searching for something to believe in, and sadly the masses eagerly gobble up the many counterfeits to fill their never ending quest for spiritual fulfillment. The religion of evolutionism with its self gratification and self worship concepts and of course, delusions of eventual evolution into god status through genocide, is clearly by far the most dangerous of the numerous counterfeit religions.

Religion really is a byproduct of something else. Although Dawkins failed to pinpoint exactly what that something else actually was, I believe that it can be pinpointed. I would ask you to consider this very simple but accurate explanation of why people gravitate toward religion. This may sound over simplified but people embrace religion or religious behavior for one of two reasons, either to avoid pain and/ or to gain pleasure. I could elaborate but if I simply toss out the idea of the stick and the carrot analogy being the motivational force behind human behavior, it should suffice. It really is that simple. Please ponder all of the many reasons that motivate people to conform to a certain belief system. I am sure you can think of many examples of why religious people, especially the extremists, seem to be so committed to their religion. Examining religious behavior, you will trace the motivational factor down to the stick and/ or the carrot eventually. Pain and/ or pleasure simply inspire people to their religious behavior, so I will not ramble on with my many examples of religious behavior being motivated out of these two powerful forces.

People tend to use religion as medicine to dull life's pain or lack of spiritual fulfillment. It's easy to equate this to a person taking doses of aspirin for chronic headaches. It is not an aspirin deficiency that causes their headaches; it may be a hydration or nutrition issue, or possibly exposure to toxins that is causing their headaches. The aspirin is not the cure, it merely treats the symptoms. An aspirin deficiency is simply not the cause of their headaches. Religion in many cases is the aspirin for the headache of estrangement from the one true living God. We all have a truth deficiency, and unfortunately many of us will medicate this inherent need for the truth with religion. We mask our need for a relationship with God with a religious aspirin. Sadly, many people never discover the root cause of their headache. Truth is the only cure for this nagging headache. The inherent need to worship a god or to ponder one's afterlife is not the result of some sort of evolutionary process called natural selection. This need is as much by design as is a molecule or a galaxy. Everyone worships something or someone, no one is without a god, they may pretend that they don't have a god, but they do have a god, and they worship their god with religious loyalty. Some may choose to appoint themselves as their own god, but they are still attempting to fill their inherent need to give praise, worship and glory to God.

Truth Quest

Since I spent much time and effort dismantling Mr. Dawkins' religion of evolutionism, I think that it is fitting that I would make a case for why I have the faith that I have. I do not really adhere to any denominational title. I never want to be more committed to a denominational title than to the truth. I likely do not agree with any believer on every detail, but who does? That does not make me always right and someone else wrong, that means we see it a little differently. My insights to God, the truth and the scriptures will forever have room for growth. If we sincerely agree on the core truth, then we share a common love and a common destiny. I suppose that I am content to call myself a believer. I am a Christian but reluctant to use the title, as it has been so mutilated by religion. I have complete confidence that the Holy Bible is the only "religious" book containing the path to eternal life through faith in Christ.

Don't many roads lead to heaven? No, this book, the Bible, is the only one of religion's many instructions manuals that has proven itself scientifically accurate. This scientifically accurate Bible says there is but one way to eternal life and it says that the one and only way is through Jesus Christ, Yeshua the Messiah. There are not multiple roads to eternal life. Nothing man can do, nor any rituals or rules that man can adhere to is sufficient to bridge the gap. Christ alone is that Bridge, not Mary, not Peter, not a high ranking church official. Christ alone is that One and only Bridge to the Father. Christ alone is the only Bridge to eternal life. "Christians" that pray in any name other than Jesus/ Yeshua, are not trusting the wisdom of God, but they are trusting in the "wisdom" and traditions of religious men. Please hear me, any person who believes in a Creator and thinks that any old road will eventually take them into eternal life. Beware that the path to eternal life is narrow, notice that I wrote path and not paths. The path to destruction is broad. Take that to mean one truth, many false religious ideologies.

I am not going to tell you that I have thoroughly studied the Koran or the teachings of Buddha or the book of Mormon, however, I do know enough about them to be certain that they are flawed, they contain information that is just not scientifically accurate. No Mohammad, the sun does not sink into a pond of murky water every evening, and no Joseph Smith, there are no Quakers living on the moon. Keep in mind that I am writing this book in an effort to illuminate the errors in the religion of evolutionism and to expose Dawkins as the prophet for profit that he is. I did not set out to expose the obvious flaws in other religions. If your curiosity is getting the best of you, I would encourage to just google "flaws in"... whatever religion you are curious about. Weigh the information, the sources and credibility and draw your own conclusions. Granted, religious denominations claiming to be Christian are among the flawed, however, it is possible for flawed denominations of Christianity to have true believers in them. God examines one's heart, not the articles of faith put together by the leaders of their church or denomination. I am not saying that diversities in one's interpretation or expression of the scriptures disqualifies them either, again, it really is a heart issue.

I am afraid that the perfect congregation does not exist on this present earth, because man is involved, and where men are involved, there sin is (self included). Christ is perfect. Christ is perfecting those who trust Him. Some unbelievers love to look for any sin in the life of someone who loves the Lord and say ah ha, you sinned, and therefore I feel justified in not believing. If your excuse for dismissing God is the sins of others, you should know that this excuse, nor any other excuse will exempt you from eternal torment in a place called hell.

I have studied in some depth, the Holy Bible and I have studied in some depth the textbooks that teach the religion of evolutionism, as well. The irony is, I studied the science textbooks believing they were true, only to later learn that they contained many lies, and I read the Holy Bible believing that it was wrong, only to learn later that it was the truth. We have all examined the evidence and after much resistance on the part of the evolutionist, we have all concluded (when caught being honest) that intelligent design is the process by which we have ended up here on planet earth in these human bodies. Did God do it? Or did aliens do it? Should I even address the faith in alien's scenario? Any encounters with little ET like, bug eyed, telepathic wizards that can abduct people into another dimension, or harvest the blood and organs of mutilated cattle, only bolsters the Bible's credibility. Demonic interlopers do in fact exist. I will elaborate on ET in chapter eight.

What makes me so sure that my God is the one true living God? Why is my chosen faith the right one? Fair questions... I decide what to believe as true or false by weighing the evidence, then figuring out what makes the most sense based upon that evidence, and then drawing a conclusion. I will not touch on the metaphysical reasons as yet, because they cannot be tangibly presented to the skeptic as evidence. My attempts to discredit the Bible backfired on me with persuasive evidence that the Bible really is God's instruction manual to mankind. The reason for my confidence in Christ Jesus being the Creator of this earth and mankind is based first on faith, but strongly backed by science. Overwhelming mathematical evidence and the scientific accuracy in the Bible gives me this unshakable faith in these scriptures. The fact that these scriptures point to the one and only bridge to eternal life being Jesus / Yeshua has convinced me that Christ is exactly Who He claimed to be, the Son of God. After critically weighing the evidence, I have full confidence in the validity of the scriptures. Please refer back to chapter one of this book, under *Sagan Studied the Prophets?*, for some of the many examples of the Bible being stunningly accurate on scientific matters, millennia before "science" would figure it out. There is not one flaw or error contained in the scriptures. Flaws in the King James Version of the Bible simply do not exist. God's word has been miraculously and perfectly preserved without error.

Examining Evidence

In order for a Bible to be published, it must be written with a 10% difference from the King James Version or any other version for that matter. When things are changed by 10%, they are no longer the same. So if you have a book that is 100% the word of God and it is changed by 10%, then what do you have? Well, you don't have the whole word of God anymore. Although it holds enough truth to deliver God's plan for salvation, it cannot contain the whole truth of the original. I am not condemning anyone for using one version or another, which is clearly not what their salvation is dependent upon. I want to explain why I choose to place my trust in the King James Version as the most accurate version of the Bible.

In the early 1600's King James 1, wanted to create an English translation of the Bible, so he had many Bibles that had been penned in many languages gathered up. He had the Bibles sent to three different institutions for translation. One team would translate in Oxford, one in Cambridge, and another team in Westminster. The translations were produced under the supervision of the school's professors, including Hebrew scholars. The three teams were not conspiring with one another to produce these copies. Upon completion of these translations, all the new English versions were sent to London. The results were amazing; all translations from all the languages were identical, with the exception of the pronunciation of people's names. That's a miracle! When books are rewritten over centuries, they never contain their original integrity, things get changed. Not so with the scriptures that King James had translated. What's even more amazing? Over many generations the copies were penned in many different languages and still retained their original integrity. That has just never happen with any other book. This should offer a person that is sincerely examining the evidence, a powerful persuasion.

Is the King James Version the only path to salvation? No, the truth of Christ is the only path to salvation. Many born again Bible believers use other versions. I used to use various translations myself, reasoning that the more perspectives that you can get on a topic, the better you will understand it. I believe that we need to be on guard against translations that change the message. If one version of the Bible is pulling me in a direction to believe one thing, like there is no absolute time frame for the creation, which is popular in modern versions, while the King James Version teaches a literal six day creation starting on day one, then I am going to side with the Bible that is correct. I know that many American English versions are much easier to read, but if I am getting conflicting messages out of two different versions, then I am persuaded that the King James Version has it right. It's obvious to me that many modern versions were created to accommodate billions of years, which almost the entire world got duped into swallowing. Chapter eight will really elaborate on exactly what drove that massive population duping. I believe the King James Version is the truest and most accurate version for the previously mentioned reasons and for the reasons I am about show you.

The science of equidistance letter sequencing has provided evidence that there is in fact, a signature from God contained within biblical text in the original Hebrew of the King James Version. I am not trying to tell you that there are secret prophecies encrypted in the scriptures, but there is clear evidence of a signature.

We find the word Torah, spelled out at 49 letter intervals. Rather strange. It would seem that someone has gone to some remarkable effort; and yet some argue that it is just a coincidence... and why this should happen in both Genesis and Exodus. The probability of such a coincidence has been estimated at about one in three million! Chuck Missler, *Hidden Treasures In The Biblical Text*

Please understand that this science was applied to the original Hebrew text of the King James Version. In Hebrew *Torah* means *The Law*. The books of Genesis and Exodus are the first two books of the five books that make up the Torah. In the fourth and fifth books of the Torah, Numbers and Deuteronomy, the phenomena takes place again, except this time the word Torah is spelled backwards. So we have the first and second book pointing the word Torah toward the third, or center book and we have the fourth and fifth book of the Torah pointing the word Torah backwards and again they are pointing at the third, or center book. The third, or center book is the book of Leviticus. Leviticus is the book of laws contained within the Torah, but it does not seem to have any equidistance lettering sequence at the 49 letter intervals. The book of Leviticus is encrypted at 7 letter intervals with the word

Yahweh, the Hebrew name for God. Yahweh is Who I pray to in the name of His Son Yeshua (Jesus).

When we return to reexamine the book of Leviticus, we discover that the square root of 49, 7, yields a provocative result. After the first yod, at an interval of seven, taking the next letter yields the tetragramaton, the ineffable name of God, the YHWH. It appears that the Torah always points toward the Ineffable Name of God. Chuck Missler, Hidden Treasures In The Biblical Text, Chapter two

Genesis		Exodus		Leviticus		Numbers		Deuteronomy
TORH	>>	TORH	>>	YHWH	<<	HROT	<<	HROT

I would call this nothing short of miraculous. The odds of this taking place in all five books to convey God's signature just couldn't be a chance happening. If this kind of statistical improbability favoring a God, Who had a design in mind, does not sway you to consider a Designer called God being involved, then please consider this... The evolutionist has to trust in staggering mathematical impossibilities that are stacked against evolution. Odds of 1 in a number that wraps around the universe to entertain the spontaneous generation of life. So who is really considering scientific evidence and weighing mathematical probability to draw their conclusions? It sure isn't Dawkins, strange he would have the audacity to pretend that it is the other way around. Impossible odds for evolution are the reality. Highly probable odds that the Bible is of divine origin is also reality. The evidence that this world was created simply exists. I sure wish Dawkins would apply some science to his world view. Anyone who says, *"you can't prove the Bible"*, clearly has not read Dr. Chuck Missler's book entitled *Hidden Treasures*. The book is just full of all kinds of mathematically impossible findings that illuminate a signature of a divine Designer of the Holy Bible.

There is a message from God encoded within the first 10 names listed in the Genesis genealogy. From Adam, the first man, to Noah, the genealogy is recorded. When you run all the names together, in their birth order, it forms an interesting sentence. Of course, for us to see it, translation from the original Hebrew into English is required. Look at these names and their meanings and tell me that these men conspired to purposely bring this about so they could convey a message of a plan for salvation that would remain a mystery for another 3,000 years.

HEBREW:	ENGLISH:
Adam	Man
Seth	Appointed
Enosh	Mortal
Kenan	Sorrow;
Mahalalel	The Blessed God
Jared	Shall come down
Enoch	Teaching
Methuselah	His death shall bring
Lamech	The despairing
Noah	Rest, or comfort

Man appointed mortal sorrow; the blessed God shall come down teaching, His death shall bring the despairing rest or comfort.

This sounds like the fall of man, and a redemption plan to me. This is all neat stuff, I will even go as far as to call it evidence. I mean Dawkins has not produced any neat instruction manuals with encoded messages by any of the aliens that he supposes have seated us here on earth. Here I am presenting evidence of stunning scientific accuracy in the words of the prophets (chapter one), and then taking it a step further and demonstrating the fact that mathematical impossibilities are encrypted in God's word. Get Chuck's book, there's lots more neat stuff, including phrases like *"His name Yeshua"* (Jesus), encrypted throughout. It's fascinating. There is one other book that I have read entitled *The Mystery of the Menorah ...and the Hebrew Alphabet,* authored by J. R. Church and Gary Stearman. This book also really illuminates the divine genius encoded throughout all of the scriptures.

I have another fact that I want to ask the non-believer to please consider. The odds of Jesus fulfilling all of the prophecies written in the Old Testament concerning the Messiah, like His birth place, His death on the cross and the numerous details in between has been accurately calculated by Peter Stoner.

Stoner considers 48 prophecies and says, "we find the chance that any one man fulfilled all 48 prophecies to be 1 in 10 to the power of 157, or 1 in 10,00,000,000,000,000,0 00,000,000,000,000,000,000,000,000,000,000,000 ,000,000,000,000,000,000,000,000,000,000,000,000,0 00,000,000,000,000,000,000,000,000,000,000,000,000 000,000,000,000,000,000! Evidence that Demands a Verdict, Josh McDowell

That is staggering. Who is weighing science and mathematical computations to form their world view? The evolutionist? Not hardly. All of these encryptions and messages that reiterate the teachings of the Bible and the mathematical impossibility of Jesus / Yeshua being anything less than authentic are really cool, but I am really only offering this as evidence for the non-believer. A believer in Christ doesn't need to know this stuff to be assured of a loving Creator that would sacrifice Himself on their behalf. The believer has the evidence in their heart. Encryptions inside of scientifically accurate and perfectly preserved scriptures are not the basis for my belief. I believe in Yeshua / Jesus because He lives in my heart. No doubt, this is where the skeptics will start heckling. *"Have you ever seen Jesus?"* No, I have never seen Jesus, but I have seen the effects of Jesus and I have felt His presence. I ask you, have you ever seen the wind? Show me some of it. Just because you have not seen the wind does not mean the wind does not exist. We do see and feel the effects of the wind. I am confident that Jesus is as real today as He was 2,000 years ago. I know this because I humbled myself and asked Him to redeem me, since I took that first step, He has been constantly revealing Himself to me. If you never humble yourself and receive His gift, then you will never feel what I am talking about. Likewise, if you bury yourself in a deep enough hole, you will never feel the wind blow or see the wind lifting a kite or swaying tree branches. Interesting that a wind analogy would come to mind, because the wind also has a way of destroying the strong fortresses in which men have placed their confidence.

The Case For Invitation

Why are so many loyal to the religion of evolutionism? This is very puzzling because the clear scientific facts demonstrate the sheer impossibility of evolutionary origins. So why such blind faithfulness to a baseless religion? I suppose because many are convinced that they could never qualify for an eternity in heaven or believe that perhaps they are not chosen by God. *"I am selfish, I lie, I lust, therefore I could not possibly be one of God's chosen few."* Don't buy the deceptions. God loves and accepts selfish, lying, thieving, even murdering sinners. Don't for one second believe that you have been excluded by God. This is the kind of thinking that drives people to totally reject the idea of a God, in an effort to ease a tormented conscience that believes deep down that God has rejected them. They boldly declare evolution as some kind of pay back to this "fictional character" that they are furious with. What other possibility could accurately explain the contempt and anger mustered by the atheist toward a God that they claim to believe is imaginary? God may be imaginary in the conscious mind of the atheist, but in their subconscious mind, God is the villain that has rejected them, and will ultimately condemn them, and they hate Him for it.

Mr. Dawkins, God has not rejected you, He welcomes you with open arms. Don't allow the forces of darkness to confuse you into thinking that you are not chosen and that you are some how excluded from the plan for salvation. The blood of Christ is so pure and so righteous that it is sufficient to cover the sins of all of humanity, even mine, and even yours. This is the core truth that I have been alluding to. Nothing outside the blood of Christ could make one presentable to God, this is truth. Religion is not truth. Christ, the Son of God, voluntarily crucified to make payment for the sins of humanity, raised from the dead after three days and now seated at the right hand of the Father, this is truth! *"But chances are I am not one of the chosen few, only a few are chosen, your Bible says so! "* Hold on a second, that's not the whole truth, and don't let some misguided evangelist cause you to give up.

So the last shall be first, and the first last: For many be called, but few chosen.
Matthew 20:16 NKJV

I am afraid that a lot of people read a verse like this and teach it to mean that humans are either born to burn in hell or go to heaven, and that we really do not have any influence on our eternity. That is a tragedy. This may very well be the misunderstanding that Dawkins and other atheists have fallen for and subsequently reject God. You do have a choice in the matter Mr. Dawkins. Few are chosen, that's clear. John the Baptist had the Holy Spirit when he was in the womb, you can't get much more chosen than that. But are the *"many called"* doomed for hell? That's not what the Bible says. I cannot conceive of those doomed for hell serving in Christ's kingdom. Few are chosen, true. The path to eternal life is narrow and few find it, true, not the path is narrow and only the chosen find it. The invitation is open to all of humanity, knock and the door will be opened. Both freewill and predestination are true.

For whom he did foreknow, He also did **predestinate** *to be conformed to the image of His Son,* **that he might be the firstborn among many brethren***.*
Romans 8:29 KJV

Now, I may not be a Theologian, but can we take this to mean anything except what it says? Here we have it, clear evidence that God does predestine men for a purpose. When I think of John the Baptist, the apostle Paul, or even some modern day believers with their ministries that reach and convert so many to Christ, I have to reflect on this verse and conclude that they were probably one of those predestined to be the firstborn among many brethren. Is predestination true? Obviously. Is freewill true? Obviously. What if the verse said *"that he might be the firstborn among many more predestined"*? Well, it wouldn't make too much sense, would it? This should put to rest the idea that we were either born to burn in hell or go to heaven, having no influence on the matter. You see, God's word never lies. I am afraid that many atheists are atheists because they have been mislead into believing that God has excluded them. God chose to send His Son to die on the cross for the sins of all of humanity, and is not willing that any should perish but that all would come to repentance. If you are an atheist because you believe that you are not one of the chosen few because you have a tendency toward sin, and thus you carry in your heart this *"why try, it's in God's hands"* attitude, that is causing you to reject God all together, you are not alone. I was there once. If you have never heard this before, hear it now, you are invited to fight the good fight, to knock and enter, to ask and receive. God does not speak just to hear Himself talk. God did not put extra words in the Bible just to create fluff. Consider these verses from the book of Revelation:

*And I saw the women, drunk with **the blood of the saints, and with the blood of the martyrs** of Jesus. And when I saw her, I marveled with great amazement.*
Revelation 17:6 NKJV

*"These will make war with the Lamb, and the Lamb will over-come them, for He is Lord of lords and King of kings; and those who are with Him **are called, chosen and faithful.**"*
Revelation 17:14 NKJV

In the first quote the woman is a reference to a tyran-nical religious governing empire that has oppressed and martyred believers for centuries. John, the writer of this pas-sage, seems to distinguish between saints and martyrs, as if the words are not synonymous. The latter verse refers to the Lamb of God (Yeshua / Jesus) in His conquering King mode, and with Him it seems will be different types of believers, the chosen, and the faithful. Now I am sure God is not just creating fluff for marketing purposes. The chosen and the faithful are not synonymous. This is good evidence that the *"called"* in Matthew 20:16, are not necessarily doomed for hell, at least not all of them, obviously a portion of them do answer the call. We all know that when our phone rings that someone is calling. We can either get up off of our bottoms and answer the call, or we can sit there watching TV and ignore the call. I guess that's why we refer to it as a call. A call is still a call, even when unanswered.

To answer the call is to respond to the prompting of God, Who draws all men unto Himself. Any drawing done, is not done by man's will but by God, this really is an undeserved gift, which makes refusing to answer the call so offensive. Enduring and persevering in the process of salvation is done through faithful persistence. By persevering in faith, the believer will refuse to fall away when attacked by the enemy, the believer will persist and not become choked out by the cares of the world and by the desires for wealth, which can happen according to Jesus.

The chosen, on the other hand, are the elect, those who are preordained for the purpose of reaching many. I believe that the elect may very well be locked into a done deal and perhaps could not be deceived or tempted out of their faith in God. If this is true, and I believe it is, it still would not change the fact that the invitation to receive Christ is open to all of humanity. It does not change the fact that the atoning power of the righteous blood of Christ is sufficient to cover the sins of all of humanity, and is in no way limited. I find it hard to fathom that any believer could put limits on the precious blood of the perfect Savior. Nothing about my Lord is limited, everything about the Lord is infinite. The apostle Paul seems to hold this view that the saints are not synonymous with the faithful. Read this greeting that Paul wrote to the church in Ephesus...

*Paul, an apostle of Jesus Christ by the will of God, **to the saints** which are at Ephesus, **and to the faithful in Christ Jesus:***
Ephesians 1: 1. KJV

Paul knows exactly what's up, he was not confused, he was not creating fluff. Paul was addressing the saints as well as the faithful. Knowing that God is not a liar, I have no other option but to believe that election is true and that freewill is also true. Can people believe for a period of time, be on the road to Salvation and then lose faith? According to the scriptures they can.

But he that received the seed into stony places, the same is he that heareth the word, and anon with joy receiveth it; Yet he hath not root in himself, but dureth for a while: for when tribulation and persecution ariseth because of the word, by and by he is offended. He that received seed among the thorns is he that heareth the word; and the care of this world, and the deceitfulness of riches, choke the word, and he becometh unfruitful.
Matthew 13: 20 - 22 KJV

So if someone is saved by grace through faith, when does their salvation become complete? When they endure to the end.

*And because iniquity shall abound, the love of many shall wax cold. **But he that shall endure unto the end, the same shall be saved.***
Matthew 24: 12-13 KJV

*But we are not of those who draw back to perdition, but of those who **believe to the saving of the soul.***
Hebrews 10:39 NKJV

I did not write these verses on my own to conform to my beliefs, this is God's word and I do not make the rules. Enduring to the end to be saved can only mean that enduring to the end will save you. These are the vast majority of believers that are the called and faithful. Many people believe that when they confess Jesus that they are locked into a done deal, not the case, that could lead to a dangerous laxness on the part of the believer. This is not some kind of "on again / off again" salvation. Sin does not cancel one's salvation. If it did, who could stand? Unconfessed sin does not cancel one's salvation. God is just, and slow to anger. If a believer were to stop loving God, and stop believing God, this is when the status of "believer" reverts to the status of "unbeliever". If that person is you right now, I ask you to please consider Jesus' analogy regarding the prodigal son in reference to the kingdom of heaven...

After striking out on his own, and finding himself lost on the road that leads to death, the prodigal son realized that he had been a fool, and that he was actually perishing in this lost state. It finally dawned on him that serving his father was the path to life, while serving himself was the path to death. He made the decision to stop being selfish and stubborn, and to humble himself before his father. This is when he returned to his father's house. His father welcomed the young man with open arms and he actually celebrated the prodigal's return with a feast. The prodigal son's brother, whom had stayed obedient to the father, questioned his father's motives for throwing a party. The following verse sums up how the father explained his actions...

*It was right that we should make merry and be glad, for your brother was **dead and is alive again**, he was **lost and is found**.*
Luke 15:32 NKJV

Of course it is best that one would never leave the road to eternal life, forsaking the safety and security of the Father's love, but if you have, and you have realized that you are dead and lost, come home. Become found, become alive again. We need to put on the full armor of God so that we will be able to stand our ground against the schemes of the enemy. If eternal security is for the believer in Jesus, and I believe it is, then it could only apply to the elect, chosen saints that have been preordained by God to be the firstborn among many other believers.

*For false Christs and false prophets shall rise, and shall shew signs and wonders, **to seduce, if it were possible, even the elect**.*
Mark 13:22 KJV

*To the general assembly and **church of the firstborn, which are written in heaven**, and to God the Judge of all, **and to the Spirits of just men made perfect**,*
Hebrews 12:23 KJV

Are the firstborn whose names are written in heaven synonymous with those men whose spirits were perfected by grace through enduring faith? Obviously not. Jesus authors the faith of the elect, while Jesus perfects the faith of the called. Many are called, few are chosen. He is the Author and Perfector of our faith. Authoring those names *"written in heaven"*, while finishing those *"Spirits of just men made perfect"*.

... Looking unto Jesus, the author and finisher of our faith, who for the joy that was set before Him endured the cross, despising the shame, and has sat down at the right hand of the throne of God.
Hebrews 12: 2 NKJV

... having made known to us the mystery of his will, according to His good pleasure which He purposed in Himself, that in the dispensation of the fullness of the times He might gather together in one all things in Christ, both which are in heaven and which are on earth - in Him.
Ephesians 1: 9-10 NKJV

Please understand, I am not trying to win an argument or a debate, I am only trying to win souls. The idea that we have been predetermined for heaven or hell causes people to give up the hope of eternal life, and cast their lots with the team that they believe that they have been assigned to. No amount of stubborn loyalty to any doctrines of men can change what the scriptures are clearly conveying to those who are honestly searching and praying for the answer to this puzzling question. I believe that I fall into the category of the vast majority of believers that are saved by grace through enduring faith. Of course it is God's goodness that draws us to Him. Everyone at some point is convicted that they need to pursue a relationship with God, some refuse to respond to this drawing, while some will absolutely, fully rebel against this drawing. Some believers are elect and some believers come by faith, endure to the end, and are saved. Don't let anyone convince you that the invitation is not open to all of humanity. The blood of Christ is sufficient to cover the sins of all mankind and is in no way limited.

It's really a shame that this issue has split evangelicals into the two camps of election and freewill. Both election and freewill are true. My intent when I embarked on writing this book was not to preach, but to debunk evolutionism and expose Dawkins as the prophet for profit that he is. So how did I wind up way out here in church sermon land? Well, I wanted to encourage the atheists, who deep down know there really is a God, but reject Him out of their thinking process in an effort to comfort their conscience which is in torment because they believe that they have been excluded by God. I want the atheist to consider the fact that God has not rejected them. If you are still breathing, you have an opportunity to be adopted into God's family.

Someone who has gone to the extreme on election is going to accuse me of taking authority away from God, by implying that we have a choice in the matter of our eternal destiny. I will make this clear, we do have a choice in the matter. If someone is telling you that the atoning blood of Christ is limited and not sufficient to cover the sins of all humanity, then they are mistaken. The blood of Christ is so holy and so pure, that it is sufficient to take away the sins of the entire world.

The forces of darkness must celebrate when they convince people that the blood of Christ is somehow limited in power. I am sure that demonic forces celebrate this deception and the diminishing of the power of Christ's blood, and they certainly celebrate the results that this confusion produces. The scriptures offer clear direction for anyone seeking eternal life through Jesus, for example, choose, confess, forsake, repent, seek, knock, ask, have faith and put on the armor of God. The scriptures are just loaded with take action verbs for anyone that is seeking salvation. If all people with eternal life through Christ were predestined, then why would these verbs need to be written? Why would the plan for salvation even need to be written? I don't know how some theologians can ignore all these verbs. Oh, so salvation is works based? Of course not, and that's not what I am saying. Nothing you did or could ever do can save you.

Please consider my brief analogy. Someone in the third world is just about to drop dead from hunger, too weak to walk, they lie there in despair waiting to die. An agent of mercy comes along with nourishing, life giving food, and spoon feeds it into the mouth of that dying person. That dying person has two options; one, they can eat the food and live; or two, they can reject that food and die. If the person eats and lives, the fact that they are alive is not because of any heroism or works on their part, they simply chose life by receiving what was being offered to them. By the same token, if that desperate, starving person rejects the food and hates the agent of mercy offering it, that would in no way incriminate the agent of mercy. Jesus/ Yeshua is the bread of life, if one chooses to partake of this bread, then that one will be with Him forever in paradise, but if that one rejects Him, they will certainly die, and spend all of eternity in torment. I know, all of this may seem heavy to an atheist, but this is the truth, and only the truth can set you free.

All Aboard

Forcing the idea of a God out of the thought processes conveniently leaves man the god of his own destiny. It seems easy to embrace this concept when the only other alternative leaves you feeling condemned, left out or rejected by the Creator. When the volumes of evidence for intelligent design mount and as the signature of a Creator becomes glaringly evident in everything from the DNA molecule to the design of the cosmos, then the atheist is left with one sad, pathetic rebuttal... Aliens must have been the ones that placed us here, and they are the wizards responsible for the creation. I am sorry, but that is just so typical of all cults, when their predictions don't pan out, they concoct brand new fabrications to cover up their errors and stubbornly refuse to let go of their brainwashed loyalty. Now that science has proven intelligent design, the faith of evolutionism has made a desperate scramble to ET as the designer and creator of all we see.

Many atheists will swallow any counterfeit idea just as long as the idea excludes the possibility of believing in a divine Creator (which deep down they are mad at for "rejecting" them). I can sincerely relate to their pain and I understand their confusion and desperation. I was that person once, I once believed the misinterpretations of the Bible, that exclude the possibility of a freewill, believing that men were born predestined to either burn in hell or be granted eternal life. Since I had an interest in girls, drugs and rock & roll as a teen, I simply concluded that I must be one of those born for the purpose of burning in hell, and if that's what God had predestined for me, then heavy metal rock stars would be my gods and I would smoke dope religiously, figuring that I might as well embrace my predetermined destination. This belief that God had excluded me would eventually cause me to reject the idea of a God all together. I felt more comfortable by simply denying His existence, but in the back of my mind I knew there certainly must be a God (and I hated Him).

As I clearly demonstrated in the previous section, nobody has been born for the purpose of burning in hell, but to serve God and worship God, not because of our goodness or strength, but because of His goodness and strength. Jesus / Yeshua loves you so much that He died for you. He paved a path for you to receive eternal life. He has not rejected you. If this sounds like an echoing of the beginning of this chapter, that's because it is. God has not rejected or excluded you from the plan for salvation. It warrants repetition. Don't swallow the lies, embrace the truth. Do not reject His invitation. With sincerity knock, and the door will be opened, seek and you will find, in humility ask and you will receive an eternal life in the presence of the Creator of this spinning world and all the cosmos that we cannot begin to fathom or comprehend. The Creator waits with open arms for you to confess His truth. That truth will set you free, freedom from delusions, freedom from embracing lies and fairytales, freedom from the need to fabricate "data" to support a world view that you know deep down is bogus. I implore you to consider that this creation may not be the result of extraterrestrial little wizards but may be the result of a divine Creator that loves you enough to die for you. I want to make an appeal to the evolutionist to say the sinner's prayer, right here, right now in this chapter. There are no perfect words, the Lord weighs the sincerity of the heart, but perhaps a prayer like this...

Jesus / Yeshua, I believe that You are the Son of God. I believe that You gave Your Life on the cross as a sacrifice for my sins. I believe that You arose from the dead after three days. Please forgive my sins, I ask You to apply Your blood to my account to pay the price for my sins. Give me a goal or a mission, I want to serve You from this day forward. You are my Savior and my King and my God.

Just pray it. You have nothing to lose. Would it be so terrible if you do not spend eternity in hell? Eternity is a long time. You don't have to clean up your act first, you do not need to kick any sinful habits first, you just need to sincerely repent. The Lord will start the process of perfecting your faith. If you prayed the prayer expecting some kind of buzz or something magical, then you may be let down, however, some have told me that they felt this unexplainable peace, and some have told me they felt fear and desperation depart from them. When I prayed a prayer like this, the weight of the world was lifted from me, my broken heart was cured, my fear and sadness turned into confidence and joy. If you prayed the prayer with a sincere heart then you are now in the family of God, and only you could sever that tie, because God has promised that He will not. From now on you can pray to the Father in the name of His Son, conveying whatever is heavy on your heart and giving thanks for His goodness ... *Abba, Father, I come to You in the name of your precious Son Yeshua, Jesus ...* and then just pour your heart out. If you are too proud to do that, then you are too proud to know God. It pleases God that you would confide in Him, making noble requests of Him and thanking Him and praising Him. No problem is too big for God and no problem is too small, He wants to hear it. That is why He created mankind, so that we could have a relationship with Him. Please do not make the mistake of rejecting His will for your life and your eternity.

For God so loved the world, that he gave his only begotten Son, that whosoever believeth in him should not perish, but have everlasting life.
John 3:16 KJV

... that if you confess with your mouth the Lord Jesus and believe in your heart that God has raised Him from the dead, you will be saved.
Romans 10:9 NKJV

A Righteous Christ Vs Reckless Christians

Christ will never let you down. Christ is not a Genie in a bottle to fulfill your every whim, He knows what's best for you. If you go into this expecting instant bliss, you will be let down. The Lord promises peace in spite of your tribulations, not a life free from attacks, trials, and injustice.

*Yes, and **all** who desire to live godly in Christ Jesus will suffer persecution.*
II Timothy 3:12 NKJV

Therefore I take pleasure in infirmities, in reproaches, in needs, in persecutions, in distresses, for Christ's sake. For when I am weak He is strong.
II Corinthians 12:10 NKJV

If I had held this prescribed peace by fully leaning on Christ as opposed to my own reasoning, in the face tribulations, I could have saved myself years of heartache and pain. "Christians" will let you down again and again, but endure in spite of that. Don't let any of the self righteous, condescending, gossiping, lying "Christians" distort your perception of Who Christ is. Christ loves you enough to die for you. People, even Christians, are sinners by nature, don't make the mistake of putting divine expectations upon them. Christians often lose sight of the fact that they are fellow servants, and servants are not called to judge other servants, they all must come under the authority of their Master. When I first believed, I kind of expected attacks from unbelievers but I never dreamed that the congregation and even the clergy would be just as capable of such mean spirited, cowardly attacks. If you are a new believer, brace yourself, "Christians" will attack you. If your faith is sincere, the forces of darkness will put forth great effort to ensure that you are attacked. You will be attacked by those who you would least suspect.

Like the religious Pharisees, "Christians" will purposely hurt you, and take heed that these religious Pharisee "Christians" are the majority in many congregations. Do not let their reckless, disrespectful behavior become your excuse to reject the truth. They are but misguided weeds that grow among the wheat, in futility they attempt to acquire righteousness by choking out the vulnerable sprouts.

Is it possible that these self righteous, gossiping, back stabbers may have more blood on their hands than a death row inmate? I believe it is possible, because when one slams the door in the face of those who are sincerely trying to enter, causing them to give up on their faith, they have in essence prevented all of the missionary work that the new believer might have done. What if that new believer would have started a mission that would have fed thousands of people that were starving to death, and reached them with the gospel? It seems to me that the self righteous, back stabbing, pew warmers may unknowingly have a whole lot of blood on their hands.

Woe to you scribes and Pharisees, Hypocrites! For you are like whitewashed tombs which indeed appear beautiful outwardly, but inside you are full of dead men's bones and all uncleanness.
- Yeshua / Jesus, Matthew 22:23 NKJV

When one feels the need to condemn or betray another in order to feel righteous, it seems to me like strong evidence that their feelings of self justification or salvation is not dependent upon the shed blood of Christ. That is really sad because the righteous blood of Christ is the only thing that could ever make any of us sinners righteous in God's sight. Please dismiss any notion that someone else's sin some how makes you righteous by comparison. Likewise, do not let someone deter your zeal for Christ by trying to stifle your growth with some unhealthy competition for righteousness or biblical intellect. Sadly for many, church is show biz, a social club or an occupation and the result is that they can be just as reckless with fragile people's feelings as those greed crazed rats in the rat race of the business world. Can you imagine a brother or sister in Christ being so consumed with making one of their domestic "brethren" feel miserable, betrayed and rejected, while at the same time having no concern or compassion for those "brethren" abroad being imprisoned, martyred and starved to death for their faith? Can you imagine this person being a legitimate brother or sister in Christ? Nor can I. These types of "Christians" are the vast majority in Christianity. It is no wonder that the unbelievers scoff.

Many on the fence seekers have been so hurt by these kinds of Pharisee "Christians" that they tend to go on the offense, looking for any hypocrisy in a Christian that may sincerely have their best interests in mind. News flash, we are all hypocrites, we all know that sin is wrong, and we continue sinning anyway. We are not sinless, but we are forgiven. We will be sinners for the rest of our lives on this earth, during this process of salvation. We are being refined until the day we die, when our faith is fully perfected, and our salvation is complete. One day the ultimate Judge will declare believers righteous in His sight, not because of any righteousness mustered on our part, but because we have the blood of the Lamb applied to our account. This ultimate Judge grants the believer an eternity in His kingdom. No excuses will work. No nasty, back stabbing pew warmers will be an excuse for uncovered sin. Only the shed blood of

Christ applied will suffice as payment. Professing **Believers**, do not become weeds that choke out any of these new sprouts. They need love, grace, mercy and forgiveness just as much as you do, so why would you withhold it from them? Where would you be without mercy and grace?

Let us not become conceited, provoking one another, envying one another.
Galatians 5:26 KJV

And let us consider one another in order to stir up love and good works.
Hebrews 10:24 KJV

Unbelievers, do not reject God's plan for your eternity because of what mean people that go to Christian churches may do to you. The road can be rough, but don't let it break you, let it build you, let it draw you into a firmer stance on the Rock of salvation.

Thy will be done

Oh Lord, You know I've had enough,
can't taste another bitter cup.
So much stress, injustice, misery,
none the less, Thy will be done in me.

Thy will be done,
Thy will be done,
Thy will be done in me.

Darkened skies and pounding rain,
can't hide the tears, can't mask the pain.
My eyes are blind to all You see,
Lord, help me find Thy will for me.

Thy will be done,
Thy will be done,
Thy will be done in me.

Waves of betrayal come crashin' down,
can't catch my breath, don't let me drown.
Lord, give me faith to walk this sea,
back to the Rock, secure in Thee.

Thy will be done,
Thy will be done,
Thy will be done in me.

-Chris Eckstein

Yes, I wrote these lyrics, but since I cannot carry a note
in a wheelbarrow, maybe some high speed, musical talent
could tune up these lyrics.

Chapter Six

Why be Moral?

My Father's House

"The other reason why you might need religion to be moral is that you are either afraid of God, your afraid if your not moral you'll get punished, or you are trying to suck up to God and be good so that you will get a reward. Neither of these two is a very noble reason to be good."
Richard Dawkins, *The God Delusion Debate*

I do not know if Dawkins has children but he seems totally unable to grasp the concept of the father, child relationship. The scriptures time and again compare the parental relationship of earthly fathers and their children, with the relationship of the heavenly Father and the child of God.

When my first son was three years old, he hadn't had any life experiences that taught him that playing in a 45 MPH street can be dangerous and deadly. I lived at the corner of International Speedway and the beach in Daytona at the time, and these seedy streets are always jumping. Since I did not want my son to have to experience getting hit by a car to realize the dangers, I warned him, if I ever saw him walking close to that street again without mom or dad that he would be getting a spankin'. He knew what a spanking was because he had received them before as a remedy to cure temper tantrums. Was my son all of the sudden terrified of me? No, although he was too immature to comprehend the dangers of getting hit by a car or the reality of being snatched up by a stranger, he was not too immature to know that disobedience would bring pain upon himself. I never had to spank him for disobeying that particular instruction. My son never got hit by a car, and he was never abducted. I like the result.

My children have some healthy fear of me, but their love for me is far greater than any fear of me. A child needs a healthy fear of their parent; this keeps them from dying before they reach kindergarten. Psych medications have proven ineffective in correcting neglect induced, behavioral disorders in undisciplined children. In my opinion, at least 90% of psych med prescriptions are unwarranted, and ultimately do more harm than good. Drugging a child may seem like a quick fix, but that is not the remedy prescribed in the Bible. This is not an area in life where you can afford to take a short cut or cheat. There simply is no magic pill that gives a child the qualities of respect, consideration, compassion or honesty. It takes a greater love for one's child than for one's self to implement corporal punishment, as needed, with love being the only motive. The following verse is one of several verses that does clearly stress the need for earthly parents to love their children enough to discipline them.

He who spares the rod hates his son, But he who loves him disciplines him promptly.
Proverbs 13:24 NKJV

This is a powerful indictment. If you neglect to implement corporal punishment, that not only means you don't
love your child, this means you actually hate your child. The
word of God implies that to neglect to discipline a child is
placing them on a road to death. No parent or guardian who
loves their child would place them on a road to death. This
next verse is in reference to the heavenly Father's love for
His children. I find it easy to see a parallel. In both cases
proper discipline is motivated out of sincere love.

*But if you are without chastening, of which all have become
partakers, then you are illegitimate and not sons.*
Hebrews 12:8 NKJV

If a child has no fear of their guardian and manages to
make it to adulthood, they will likely have no consideration
for others and no regard for the rule of law. A childhood with
no fear of an authority that will impose consequences for
bad behavior, is almost certain to produce an angry, narcis-
sistic, rebellious youth. Over 70% of prison inmates grew up
in a home without a father to implement loving discipline.
If there is no male father figure in the family to implement
correction, then you are going to have to step up and make
the behavior adjustments mom. I know that spanking a child
can be more painful for the one administering the spanking
than it is for the child, so it is easy to search for excuses to
not do it. This is what I mean by loving the child more than
yourself. It makes you feel better for the moment to skip
over corporal punishment, but this robs the child of healthy
boundaries. If a spanking is painless it will become a joke to
the child, and it will not be too long before your authority is
a joke to that child, as well. Your child is way too important,
you can't risk your child growing up to believe that rebellious behavior is without painful consequences, and ultimately hating you for it. Likewise, my heavenly Father has

instilled in me that rebellious behavior is not without consequences. The heavenly Father loves me enough to give me strong incentives to want to stay off of the road that leads to death, and stay on the road that leads to life. God loves me, and He is just to forgive me, but that does not change the fact that certain behavior is not without certain consequences.

The respect that is generated by a certain amount of fear is healthy. Like my sons, I love my Father and try to do His will, which is to avoid sin. If I do sin, it hurts Him, which in itself hurts me. I do not want to hurt my Father. I do not want to make light of the fact that it is my sin that nailed my Savior to the cross. I cannot get comfortable living in a way that brings heartache to my Father. I know that I do sin and I know that it hurts God, that's why I really try not to sin. Is sucking up to God to get a reward my motive? No, I have been granted the wisdom to understand that sin causes pain. I feel that there is enough pain in the world. My sin not only hurts me, it also hurts others as well. I am so tired of hurting others. I still recklessly slip from time to time, but it is always followed by regret. I have always reasoned that it is easy to love people, but if they hurt me for no reason, then I am going to pay them back. It's hard for us humans to let go of the desire to punish someone who has hurt us, especially when they do this by hurting those we love. God requires His children to forgive and pray for those who hate you and attack you without cause. My biggest down fall has been not heeding this command. This is a good opportunity for me to apologize to anyone that I may have hurt. If you are reading this and I have hurt you... I want to say that I am sorry, and please forgive me if I have sinned against you. Since I first believed, I have gradually sinned less and less. This is a refining process that will continue until the day I die.

Any son of mine, whether biological or adopted has a home with me. Since he is my son, my home will always be open to him, no matter how bad he messes up, and no matter how big his mistakes are. My son can always find refuge and unconditional love in his father's house. He is my son, and I am his father, he is always welcome in my home. If my son wanted to leave me, I wouldn't try to stop him, but like the father of the prodigal, I would be waiting, watching and praying for his safe return. I want him to stay with me because I know that this is the best and safest place for him. He is not sucking up to me, he is my son, and he loves me. Dawkins may believe that I am sucking up to God, but I say that I love my Father Who has done so much for me, and I never again want to be estranged from His love. Is Dawkins trying to assess relationships that he is not qualified to assess, or is he just trying to belittle someone for believing that their Creator is more than just a little space alien? That is less than noble of Dawkins.

After having referenced God in the ways that I have thus far in this chapter, I feel strongly compelled to offer the reader an explanation of this Triune God. Is God one, or is God three? God is One. How then can one God have three different components? He can, He's God (I just said that to get Richard's goat). Here's how, imagine a huge sea of crystal clear living water. That is God the Father. Now imagine a fountain flowing from that sea of living water, giving refreshment to a dry, parched land, but still very much a part of that source. That is Jesus / Yeshua, the Son. Now imagine you, being permitted to bathe in or drink of this living water, that's the Holy Spirit. One who thirsts, can trust Christ to give them forever quenching living water. Yeshua / Jesus is the fountain of living water. Consider the three aspects of this great big sea of water when trying to fathom a Holy Trinity. Look at yourself for example, you are composed of mind, body and spirit, but you are still one person. Water can take the form of liquid, solid or gas, but it remains water. The analogies are plentiful. The Lord, our God is One.

Ante Up

As a former gambling man, I had to ask myself, is trusting in God worth it? Of course it is. I have everything to gain and nothing to lose. Now that is a safe bet. If I am wrong, then I have lived my life praying to a God who isn't there, finding strength through faith and hope, finding joy by serving those in need. If I am wrong and this God thing is bogus, then I die and get recycled as a daisy or a dung beetle. What have I lost? Nothing, in fact, the lifestyle that I have lived since coming to Christ has given me a Lord in Whom I can take refuge in during times of pain or sorrow. I am now experiencing the joys of marriage and children. I did not have these sources of real joy and contentment in my previous life as a God denier. I am much happier with this blessed hope. I no longer need to be apprehensive about my life's future, nor do I need to fear my afterlife. If I am wrong about all this, then what have I lost? And why would me trading my former lifestyle for this much safer and more stable lifestyle make me ignorant, insane or stupid? Can't I just *"dance to my DNA"* in the way that works for me, Richard? Why would you insult someone who is just trying to find peace and joy the best way they know how? So what if I am wrong? What I have lost? Nothing!

The atheist on the other hand has placed an enormous bet against infinite odds with nothing to gain and everything to lose. The atheist can religiously reject God, ridicule people who believe in God, and even publicly sing John Lennon songs praising atheistic ideology. Sooner or later that atheist, like everyone else, is going to cash in their chips. What if the atheist is wrong? What if there is a God? Then the atheist will spend eternity in hell. Unfathomable torment, indescribable suffering, extreme rage, confusion, frustration, hate, excruciating pain and agony that has no end. That is hell. Hell is not some party with a keg of Heineken and all your friends lounging around pumping the tap. Hell is eternity estranged from the peace, love, joy and euphoria that God has offered humanity. If salvation through Christ is a falsehood, then I guess it really doesn't matter, but if salvation through Christ is true, then it matters big time. What if Dawkins is the one who is mistaken? What if Dawkins is the one who is wrong, then what has he lost? Everything!

A Short Biography

Dawkins himself explains that as a child he went from believing in God to disbelief in God and for period of time during his teen years, he went back to believing in God, and then finally wrote God off all together. I am paraphrasing, but that pretty well sums up Mr. Dawkins' testimony that he gave during the introduction to the God Delusion debate with John Lennox in Birmingham, Alabama in October, 2007. Let me give you my interpretation of why Mr. Dawkins had this reluctant slip into the religion of evolutionism...

As a child Dawkins attends public schools where they hammer him with the religion of evolutionism day in and day out. Whether Dawkins realizes it or not, the teachers serve as role models. Even on a conscious level Dawkins emulates those who he spends time with. I would suspect that Dawkins spent about 30 hours a week learning in a public school. He is being taught that the earth is billions of years old and that the universe and humans are the result of evolutionary processes. Dawkins spends one or two hours a week in a church that was probably very boring for him, he probably had to wear his uncomfortable Sunday best cloths to church. He probably would rather have been outdoors playing, pedaling his bicycle to the corner store to blow his allowance on rubbish such as penny whistlers and moon pies. Who can blame him, church was probably boring, and we all know how repulsive self righteous, holy rollers can be. I believe that it was easy for the young boy Dawkins to conclude that church was the most boring of all his child-hood activities. Dawkins probably lumped God in with the less than pleasant visits to the church.

After reaching his teens, an age appropriate in which to be held accountable for foolishness, Dawkins has a reemerging realization that there is in fact a God. We all feel this inner voice telling us that committing robbery, rape and murder is wrong. This is not due to a misfiring in some pro-cess of natural selection, this is a product of design called the conscience. Morality is written on the tablets of our hearts, and it tells us that there is a God. Certainly with persistence, one can become numb to or void of this inner truth that God has placed within the heart of men; you could call it searing one's conscience. A conscience is placed in every man, both believer and non believer. When a person commits a partic-ular sin for the first time, it always feels wrong, but after the sin continues and the evil goes unchecked, one's conscience can be seared to the point that the person no longer hears the small voice inside, and they can actually become quite comfortable committing rapes or murders. The conscience is not a product of natural selection as atheists purpose. The conscience is placed in man by God, and it is that very con-science that tells us that there is a God, and that He will one day hold us accountable. Searing the conscience not only allows people to commit hideous acts without remorse, but it can also allow people to deny the God that their conscience once told them was real.

Dawkins arrives on the scene in college. Here Dawkins is made to feel that if he believes in God, he is not intelligent, and we all know that unintelligent people do not make good grades. But good grades are needed in order to get the money and the girl. His professors who have the obvious psychological and academic edge over him, make Dawkins feel like an ignorant moron if he does not swallow Darwinian evolutionism. Dawkins, both on a conscious and a subconscious level, desperately wants to make good grades and believes that being like the professors will help him to realize this desire. This is where the suck up kicks into high gear. A suck up of such magnitude that it can actually redirect a rational thinking process. Know that 75% of faith professing students who go to secular colleges will denounce their faith within one year, now that's staggering. That's why it's very important, mom and dad, that you select a college or university for your child that does not practice lies, deception and communistic style indoctrination methods to convert young people to their religion. In Dawkins' effort to polish the big apple, and eat the big cheese, he crumbles like a soda cracker in a cat 5 hurricane. Dawkins claims to swallow the evolutionism scheme, hook, line and sinker. Now he is educated, now he is one of the deep thinkers, now he is a pillar of academic excellence... He has rejected God! It sounds humorous enough, but when you consider the fact that it happens time and again every single day, it really is kind of sad, especially when you consider the blood drenched history of Darwinian evolutionism. As a boy Dawkins attempted to reject God. As a teen his inner voice declares that there is a God, but in spite of that bout with his conscience, Dawkins still manages to reject God.

And for this reason God will send them strong delusion, that they should believe a lie.
II Thessalonians 2:11 NKJV

I have heard Dr. Kent Hovind quote this Bible verse on occasion and add, *"Anyone that thinks they evolved from a rock 4 billion years ago is strongly diluted. It takes years of conditioning to get people to believe something so silly."* My guess is that this statement offended Dawkins so much that he responded by entitling his next book *The God Delusion*. In this role of spin doctor, Dawkins invites his audience to ingest the idea that belief in creation is some kind of psychotic delusion.When you take a close look at a person that is willing to suck up for reasons of advancing their own agenda, without exception that person enjoys being sucked up to. I suppose the rationale is; I had to suck up, now it's your turn, suck up to me, so I can feel powerful. So, Dawkins forges on to become a professor, along the way Dawkins encounters many obstacles to his belief system, but he persists on with the delusion. He has way too much invested by this time to cop out of his religion. Now he is a high priest, now he can distort the young minds that are psychologically and academically inferior to him, now he is in driver's seat. In his mind he must seem like, well, a god to these students. Over the decades, the evidence for evolution crumbles, yet he holds fast to the ideology that has made him rich and famous. As the scientific evidence for intelligent design continues to mount, Dawkins refuses to buckle. He is a star now and to concede to the scientific evidence that God designed this creation would mean giving up his super star status, or so he thinks (actually Dawkins confessing the truth would bring him more recognition than he has ever known). Blindly bound by faith in the religion of evolutionism, in where he believes he holds the status of famed, brilliant scientist, he just cannot find it within himself to release his anti-God fanaticism, in spite of the overwhelming evidence. Ignoring science is no longer sufficient, Dawkins will have to embrace science fiction in order to patch all the holes in his religion, and little alien wizards may just be the patches that he needs to plug all of these holes. Dawkins' seared conscience will not budge in the face of clear evidence of intelligent design. On a positive note, anything that man can do, God can undo. Could God unsear Dawkins' conscience? God could, and I hope He does. That could only happen if Dawkins humbles himself before the Lord. It couldn't hurt for Dawkins to concede that John Lennon telling him to imagine no God really isn't as cool as it seemed to be 40 years ago. But hey, I can relate, when I was young I thought that rocks stars had all the answers; they certainly had the money and the super models. I am forced to ponder why an evolving man like Dawkins would not have evolved beyond this adolescent phase by now. I sincerely hope that Dawkins realizes how pathetic he looks when, after decades of preaching that life created itself, he purposes that aliens could be the divine designers. Earth to diluted one? Earth to diluted one? Do you read me?

Chapter Seven

Unchanging Truth

The Immoral Man

Nice Christians will have been protesting throughout this section: everyone knows the Old Testament is pretty unpleasant. The New Testament of Jesus undoes the damage and makes it all right. Doesn't it?
-Richard Dawkins *The God Delusion*

It seems clear to anyone who has read the Bible, that Dawkins has not read the Bible. Dawkins has successfully excerpted any verses that he could find to demonstrate the sinful nature of men, reasoning that since these lovers of God were sinful, then that means their God must not exist. Since Dawkins obviously has not comprehended the Bible, I will clear it up for him. All men are sinners, their hearts are desperately wicked, with one exception. That one exception is Yeshua. Dawkins finds all kinds of sin stains on the men of the Bible, but failed to find one sin that Jesus committed, yet still manages to miss the whole point of the book. In a nutshell, I will clear up the confusion for Dawkins. Richard, men are sinful, in need of salvation. Jesus is the perfect

Savior, the Son of God, the Son of man, who lived a flawless life and offered Himself as a sacrifice to pay the price for the sins of humanity, my sins and yours. I am sorry you missed that.

The God of the Old Testament is the same God of the New Testament. Jesus is not a change from the Old Testament, read the book, Jesus is a fulfillment of the Old Testament. Understand that the God of the Old Testament did not cease to exist when Jesus arrived as a man on earth. I wish I could enlighten Dawkins. I could not even begin to explain the relationship between the story of Abraham almost sacrificing his son on the alter (by faith believing God would raise him from the dead), and the death of the Son of God on the cross to someone who does not believe the fundamental message. For me to do that would be like trying to describe the color purple to a person who was born blind. I could not begin to explain the significance of the Passover in relation to the crucifixion of the Lamb of God to someone who has hardened their heart toward the truth. It would be like me attempting to describe the sound of a flute to a deaf person. In order for a candle to light a dark room, the candle must first be lit. To revere the Lord is the very beginning of understanding.

The fear of the LORD is the beginning of wisdom, And the knowledge of the Holy One is understanding.
Proverbs 9:10 NKJV

The Old Testament seems *"just plain weird"* to Dawkins. In all honesty, in a lot of places, the Old Testament seems just plain weird to me too. That does not change Who God is. Some of the pages in a calculus book would seem just plain weird to a preschooler too, I suppose. Consider God and His infinite wisdom and then consider man and his limited understanding. To say that God's wisdom is the Pacific ocean and that man's understanding is a speck of mist, is to understate God's wisdom. I do not claim to have even an inkling of the complexity of God, nor can I begin to fathom His mysterious ways. Still I beg for any proof that should get me to doubt His existence. I beg you for any proof that should give me cause to consider any possibility of evolution. Creation Science Evangelism has been offering $250,000 for proof of evolution for over 10 years, but no enlightened scientist has stepped forward to claim the prize. You see, there is NO proof for evolution that would make a case in a court of law. Evolutionism is founded upon fairytales, theories and circular reasoning.

Dawkins' ability to point out transgressions of the biblical men who loved God, is actually supportive of the Bible's teaching that men are sinful and in need of a Savior. Surprise, Dawkins failed to find any blemish on Christ. Dawkins is without any accusation against Christ because Christ is sinless. Dawkins failed to point out any scientific inaccuracies in the either of the Testaments. Dawkins also failed to find any falsehoods in either Testament. There is a reason. I will never begin to understand or pretend to understand God and all of His ways. I do understand Him enough to know that humanity is sinful, desperately wicked, and that we all fall short of deserving God's mercy and grace. We are all in need of redemption. Our awesome Creator has provided us with just such a plan for redemption. He has offered us Himself, a perfect, sinless sacrifice to pay the penalty for our sins.

The Moral Savior

Indeed Jesus, if he existed (or whoever wrote his script if he didn't) was surely one of the great ethical innovators of history.
Richard Dawkins *The God Delusion*

It certainly is convenient for Dawkins to doubt the existence of Jesus, but he never doubts the existence of men in the Bible that did questionable acts thousands of years prior to the human presence of Christ on earth. A weak way to make a case. Dawkins concedes that the precepts taught by Jesus are ethical. Thank you for your honesty, Richard. Yet again Dawkins demonstrates how the scriptures are not comprehendible to an unbeliever. Dawkins insists that Jesus taught from scripts. Jesus would not have needed a script, if Dawkins had read the introduction to the book of John, he would know that Jesus, in the flesh, was actually the Word of God, incarnate...

In the beginning was the Word, and the Word was with God, and the Word was God. The same was in the beginning with God. All things were made by him; and without him was not anything made that was made. In him was life; and the life was the light of men. and the light shineth in the darkness, and the darkness comprehended it not.
John 1: 1-5 KJV

Jesus did not use a script; Jesus is the Script. Jesus did not write one word in the New Testament, the books of this Testament were written by witnesses, that knew Jesus and witnessed His miracles, both before and after His crucifixion. The fact that their accounts come from such very different perspectives adds even more credibility to the fact that Jesus is not the product of the imaginations of men gathering to fabricate a new religion so that they could die a martyr's death proclaiming it.

Dawkins' denial of Christ's existence is a demonstration of his anti-Christian world view. Jesus is the most famous and real historical figure of all times. Dawkins is relentless in his persistent effort to persuade gullible minds of an improbability of a God, but trying to stretch that into denying the existence of Jesus, at least as a person, demonstrates his desperation to rid society of the truth. Christ Jesus is certainly the most established historical figure ever, so much in fact, that the human records of time tell of His presence on earth, BC, before Christ, and AD, after death (of Christ). I would like to encourage Mr. Dawkins to google *first century secular accounts of Jesus*. After Mr. Dawkins reads the numerous accounts of the many famous, secular, first century writers and historians that attest to the reality of Jesus, perhaps Dawkins would be inclined to retract his statements made as a result of either his extreme ignorance, or a blatant attempt to deceive. We see the classic case of stubborn denial on the part of Dawkins. Sorry, but one cannot wish Jesus out of history, no more than one can wish theists out of the founding of the United States. One can deny it, and lie about it, but that does not change the facts. The moral Teacher Jesus / Yeshua of the New Testament was not only the Word of God incarnate, He is the Son of God, the Son of man and the sacrifice for the sins of all humanity. The details of His life were predicted in the Old Testament, from His place of birth to His brutal death on the cross (long before crucifixion was even implemented), and dozens of details in between his conception and death, without one error, and against insurmountable mathematical odds. Please remember that the odds of Jesus fulfilling all of the prophecies written in the Old Testament concerning the Messiah has been calculated at 1 in 10 to the power of 157. Remember all those zeros? That is a huge number.

Dawkins The Prophet

The Ten Commandments were given to men by God, through Moses, as a moral compass, not as a means to salvation. The Ten Commandments actually clearly demonstrate that no man is without sin. Which one of us has never lied, stolen or coveted? Which one of us has never sinned? Which one of us could stand before God based on our own righteousness? Christ alone can stand on His righteousness. We could never measure up. The good news (the gospel) is that we can stand righteous, being pardoned by the atoning blood of the righteous Savior. We can measure up, based on the fact that Christ is sinless.

Dawkins holds the view that the Ten Commandments are somehow evolving. As a result of this view, Dawkins claims he typed into a search engine "New Ten Commandments". This is what Dawkins came up with.

1. *Do not do to others what you would not want them to do to you.*

2. *In all things, strive to cause no harm.*

3. *Treat your fellow human beings, your fellow living things, and the world in general with love, honesty, faithfulness and respect.*

4. *Do not overlook evil or shrink from administering justice, but always be ready to forgive wrong doing freely admitted and honestly regretted.*

5. *Live life with a sense of joy and wonder.*

6. *Always seek to be learning something new.*

133

7. *Test all things; always check your ideas against facts, and be ready to discard even a cherished belief if it does not conform to them.*

8. *Never seek to censor or cut yourself off from dissent; always respect the right of others to disagree with you.*

9. *Form independent opinions on the basis of your own reason and experience; do not allow yourself to be led blindly by others.*

10. *Question everything.*

(This was not enough for Dawkins; he had to add in four more commandments to complete his new morality code. Dawkins seems to want to be the modern day Moses, delivering new and improved moral instructions for humanity.)

11. *Enjoy your own sex life (so long as it damages nobody else) and leave others to enjoy theirs in private whatever their inclinations, which are none of your business.*

12. *Do not discriminate or oppress on the basis of sex, race or (as far as possible) species.*

13. *Do not indoctrinate your children. Teach them how to think for themselves, how to evaluate evidence and how to disagree with you.*

14. *Value the future on a timescale longer than your own.*

The Prophet Unmasked

This all sounds so wonderful, unfortunately all 14 commandments really fall short of manifesting any newly evolved deep moral revelations. Allow me to comment on the above commandments. The number on every comment will correspond with the number on every one of Dawkins' previously listed new commandments. Maybe we can have some fun dissecting these new morality codes. Lets find out what direction Dawkins' (the anti-Moses) new moral compass is really trying to lead society.

1. Do unto others? A philosophy that has been being proposed for thousands of years, and really offers no evolving insight. *Therefore, whatever you want men to do to you, do also to them, for this is the Law and the Prophets.* Matthew 7:12 NKJV

2. Strive to cause no harm, except to the unborn, newborns, non productive and elderly members of society, and perhaps those of the inferior gene pool.

3. Share the brotherly love man, unless of course, those fellow humans are not as evolved as you, then permission to perform genocide is granted. Respect all living things except for those overpopulated, carbon emitting, earth destroying sub humans.

4. Do not overlook evil, unless it is done in an effort to advance the cause of evolutionism.

5. Live oblivious to the fact that in the US, 4,500 babies will die today. Measures to implement tax funded euthanasia are fully employed. Whistle a happy tune, because you can't feel their pain.

6. Learn something new? Like the true number of dead humans crushed under the wheels of evolutionary progress?

7. Test all things, just as long as the results do not conflict with evolutionism. Piltdown and Lucy hoaxes, radiometric dating and geologic column fraud, magnetic reversal lies, ontogeny recapitulating phylogeny lies (big words, stupid theory), Pangea fantasies; this stuff may not be tested and exposed.

8. Respect others, unless they will not bow down to the golden monkey. *"It is absolutely safe to say that if you meet someone who claims not to believe in evolution, that person is ignorant, stupid or insane."* - Richard Dawkins

9. Don't be led blindly, unless it is a blind watch maker that does the leading. *Can the blind lead the blind? Shall they not both fall into a ditch?* Luke 6:39 KJV

10. Question creation, blindly follow evolutionism.

11. People's sex lives are none of your business (true). Just grin and bear it, as we high jack trillions of your grandchildren's tax dollars to fund millions of abortions and pay for the phenomenal cost of treating AIDS and other STD's as a result of atheistic lifestyles.

12. Ha ha. That's funny; Darwin was an outspoken "racist" and sexist. He encouraged the idea of evolved civilizations killing off the "savage races". Darwin declared that women are inferior to men in every way in his book, *The Descent of Man.*

13. Do not indoctrinate your children; we prefer a clean slate to work with when they are in school, so that we can do the indoctrinating.

14. Value the future by speeding up the evolution process and reducing the population of those "savage races".

Now you have seen the prophet Dawkins' Ten (Fourteen) Commandments unmasked. I thought it was only fair that we get to the true meaning behind people's motivation for declaring new and improved morality codes for humanity. The religion of evolutionism is not only the religion most lacking morality, evolutionism is actually void of any morality. I can agree that we do not need religion to be good, however, we do need the truth, and we do need to banish the insane idea that killing inferiors is somehow a path to exaltation and enlightenment. When the candy shell around the poison melts away, it has only revealed death and destruction on scales never fathomed until after the birth of the modern religion of Darwinian evolutionism.

The NWO's Ten Commandments

I could easily believe that Dawkins just added the new Ten Commandments for the purpose of creating fluff, but I am forced to wonder if Dawkins is aware of the New World Order's Ten Commandments. Is Dawkins among the millions of clueless pawns oblivious to NWO's agenda to depopulate the earth and implement a one world court and a one world religion? I really don't know, I am all but certain that he hates God, but is Dawkins really unaware of how he is being used by the forces of darkness to help usher in this NWO? I do not know if Dawkins' participation in this movement is willful or not. I do know that either way, it is spiritual forces that are driving him to promote the NWO agenda. The Georgia Guide Stones contain the true new Ten Commandments for this New World Order that Dawkins is so aggressively trying to usher in.

The Georgia Guide Stones are a replica of Stonehenge and are commonly referred to as "humanities tombstones". Take a look at the Illuminati's NWO agenda for yourself. Please youtube the words **"NWO Georgia Guide Stones"**, you will see it with your own eyes, if that does not convince you, go to Elberton, Georgia and see the NWO's Ten Commandments up close and personal. The Godless agenda is quite clear. Commandment number one calls for a scheme to reduce the earth's population by 90% (Darwinian progress). Commandment number two implements the creation of a higher level of humans through wiser reproduction (Darwinian progress). Commandment number four revokes religious freedom. Commandment number eight makes citizens into slaves to their government. The Illuminati has been working for millennia to bring about this utopia; a Satanic religion to govern the entire world. It appears that they are now closer to accomplishing this goal than they have ever been before. The Illuminati's NWO Ten Commandments are as follows...

1. Maintain humanity under 500,000,000 in perpetual balance with nature.
2. Guide reproduction wisely - improving fitness and diversity.
3. Unite humanity with a living new language.
4. Rule passion - faith - tradition - and all things with tempered reason.
5. Protect people and nations with fair laws and just courts.
6. Let all nations rule internally resolving external disputes in a world court.
7. Avoid petty laws and useless officials.
8. Balance personal rights with social duties.
9. Prize truth - beauty - love -seeking harmony with the infinite.
10. Be not a cancer on the earth - Leave room for nature - Leave room for nature.

No need to analyze this agenda, it seems pretty much straight to the point. I can't make this stuff up, and I wouldn't print it if it were not true. Youtube **"Glenn Beck threatened by NWO"**. You will see that Glenn Beck was hours away from covering a story about FEMA camps, martial law and a totalitarian NWO agenda. It seems so obvious to me that someone scared the heck out of him to get him to spin 180 degrees on the issue in a matter of hours. Glenn appears to make great efforts to appease whoever threatened him, as he sheepishly recants his statements, and nervously tries to laugh it off. See it for yourself, it is very disturbing for liberty loving individuals like me. I like Glenn Beck and his show, but it seems so obvious that he was threatened, perhaps a threat that included his family, who knows. Don't be mad at me Glenn, I love your work and agree with you on much, but in all fairness, you should respect a guy for reporting what is so clear.

I know that the previous paragraph is going to destroy any chance of me plugging my book on Fox news, although Bill O'Reilly did give Dawkins five minutes. I am committed to the truth even when it does not benefit me. You are a fair and balanced guy Bill, so give me five minutes to plug my book, just like you gave Dawkins five minutes to plug his book. I sure like Bill's show *The O'Reilly Factor*; I have been watching Bill's show for over 10 years, but I have noticed that Bill won't touch the Illuminati, it seems that Bill wants to deny their existence. This is a strong indicator to me that Bill is well aware that investigating the Illuminati can be hazardous to your health.

Tim Russert grilled both George W. Bush and John Kerry on their affiliations with the Skull and Bones secret society. Tim Russert didn't live very long after that. Coincidence? Tell that to JFK. I have seen the graphic footage of what happened to JFK after he threatened to expose the Illuminati's secret societies that are running the government, and I am not fully convinced that he died from natural causes. The Illuminati not only controls textbook content, but they also own the media.

Alex Jones has a website called **infowars.com**. What I like about Alex is that he refuses to be intimidated by the forces of the Illuminati, as he exposes their agenda. Alex actually infiltrated one of their secret meetings at the Bohemian Grove, and left with video footage of a Satanic, sacrificial ritual. Yes, the video is on youtube. Isn't it nice to know that the highest ranking United States' government officials from both sides of the isles can put aside their partisan differences and come together for some social recreation? Alex must be fully aware that his investigations and reports could cost him his life, but the truth seems to be more important to him. You've got to respect Alex Jones for his brave commitment to reporting the truth.

I know enough about history to understand that history has a way of repeating itself. Would it be too much of a stretch to suspect that depopulation atrocities could happen again? I don't think it's too much of a stretch at all, especially when you consider that it is the same god of evolutionism that has driven every single mass murder campaign. The god of evolutionism is Satan. Evolutionism is Satanism's greatest smoke screen. Evolutionists are not just simply attacking the living God, they are actually defending their god, Satan. The next chapter is going to demonstrate this revelation with detailed clarity. Buckle up, the ride isn't over yet, and it's going to get even bumpier.

Chapter Eight

Evolutionism, The Most Hostile Religion

The Origin of Feces?

When we look at the Darwinian death toll that has been inflicted on humanity, we see clear evidence that evolutionism is by far the most brutal religion of all times. Darwin's book *The Origin of Species*, spawned the most genocidal century in human history. Perhaps the book would have been more appropriately entitled: *The Origin of Feces*. Dawkins uses the following quote from Sean O'Casey in his book *The God Delusion*.

Politics has slain its thousands, but religion has slain its tens of thousands. -Sean O'Casey

The sentence would have been accurate to include, *and the religion of evolutionism has slain its hundreds of millions*. Will the real mass murderer please stand up?

Let's take a quick look at the top 5 mass murderers of all times. In all fairness, these are the most conservative estimates that I could find. Some estimates have some of these figures up to 100% higher.

1. Joseph Stalin, an atheist responsible for the death of at least 42,000,000 people.
2. Mao Tse-Tung, an atheist responsible for the death of at least 37,000,000 people.
3. Adolph Hitler, an atheist responsible for the death of at least 20,000,000 people.
4. Chiang Kai-shek, an atheist responsible for the death of at least 10,000,000 people.
5. Vladimir Lenin, an atheist responsible for the death of at least 4,000,000 people.

Source: http://freedomsnest.com/rummel_murderers.html

At least 9 of the top 10 mass murderers were atheists. It seems to me that "educators" are deliberately overlooking the correlation between mass murder and Darwinian atheism. That's still not enough, "educators" want to spin it 180 degrees and make it seem to the young student that someone who has the audacity to weigh the evidence and believe in a Creator is the villain. I do not know of one devout Darwinian professor that does not believe that he or she comes from the more highly evolved gene pool, and that they are in some way superior to the less evolved components of society. Many members of evolutionism may be totally ignorant of the death and destruction that Darwinism has spawned, so it seems perfectly fine for them to indoctrinate young minds into their religious view. Almost without exception, evolutionism's priests believe that they are of the smarter gene pool. Not all professing in evolutionism hold this smug, superiority view, but it is rampant among the "educators". Instructors want to make sure that any student that may question or reject their religion, looks and feels as dumb as they possibly can. After all, it is the evolutionism priest that will be giving the student their grade, so the professor can direct this persuasive influence at the young student with little if any rebuttal.

I bring this to light in an effort to help us better understand why these "educators" have such a high success rate in swaying young minds into the cult of evolutionism. Success is achieved by constant repetition and deceptive, communistic style indoctrination methods. Proven lies are taught to the students as fact over and over and over again. Loaded test questions (*"have humans evolved to their highest level yet, or are we still evolving?"*) are common place in science exams. Fabricated hoax, after fabricated hoax is taught as evidence for macro evolution. The secular elementary, middle and high schools serve as prep courses for evolutionism, but when the youth hits the college or university, usually away from parental guidance and reasoning, that's when the full blown religious style indoctrination machine gets turned on full throttle. It's the college "educated" mind that is more likely to reach a position of power and influence in our society. Perhaps that is one reason that evolutionism is being shoved down their throats with such force at the college level, to ensure that the religion of evolutionism continues to be financed by the tax payers.

A State Funded Religion

Why such hostility toward university professors or researchers that decipher the evidence and conclude that intelligent design is a possibility? Why are they fired or pressed out of a job? Why would rational, open minded, academic overseers oppress another opinion with such fervor? There is no rational explanation. This is clearly spiritually driven. It reeks like a rotting fish. The anger and hostility toward the idea of a Creator makes it so obvious that this is simply a case of religious gurus defending their faith.

One of Satan's greatest successes is that he has convinced people that he does not exist, and all the while pulling their strings, and igniting their fuses so they lash out at anyone that believes in a Creator. There are plenty of far out religions, granted, and it seems that everyone has a "sound reason" for believing whatever it is that they chose to place their faith in. To say that this is some battle between science and religion is to misrepresent the facts. The truth is that evolutionism and creation are competing religious ideologies. That is indisputable.

Would it be truthful to call a belief system that is built on lies and blind faith, science? "Science" has filled our textbooks with lies at every learning level, they have lied to us about the age of the earth. They have lied to us about the accuracy of radiometric dating. They have lied about a geologic column that is billions of years old. They have fabricated hoaxes to provide evidence for macro evolution. They will teach students to have blind faith in things that are not provable and highly unlikely, in many cases very disprovable. Without relent, the defenders of this faith keep pushing their religion. Time and time again they publish lies to support their theories and agendas. When it comes to debate, they want to label that pack of lies and bad theories as facts and call that science. Then lump all other forms of religion together, from Islamic Fascism to Greek Mythology, calling it religion and compete in that arena. "Science vs. Religion"? Hardly, this is very much the evolutionism religion competing against creation. Why don't we just call it "lies vs. truth"? Let's call it what it is. Shouldn't we have simple categories for considering what should be taught to the youth and printed in our "science" textbooks, especially since this is being paid for by taxpayers? Here is a suggestion for three simple categories.

Category 1- Facts: Observable, testable, measurable facts, things that can be proven by evidence and scientific laws may be admitted.
Category 2- Theory: Something we don't know but we can only hypothesize about, presenting all of the various hypothetical scenarios may be admitted.
Category 3- Fiction: Falsehoods and lies that have no place in any textbook should not be admitted (yet, they still remain today).

Please keep in mind that Category 3 is the only category in where you will find the case for evolution and the earth being billions of years old. Here's an idea, let's just teach verifiable, provable, documented facts as science. What we do not know for certain, and can only hypothesize about, this should be labeled as theory, with all views presented. That's not asking too much, is it? Evolution is a theory, and a weak theory at that, however, it is taught as if it were fact. This is not science vs. religion. This is lies vs. truth. Do you know who the father of all lies is? If we removed all the lies and labeled any theory as the theory that it is, then the textbooks would only be left with truth. So why wouldn't Darwinian "science" make that the objective? Because if they did that, then the evolutionism religion would collapse like a house of cards in a wind storm. Prophets of evolutionism have no desire to expand their thinking or deepen their understanding. This is absolute religious faith in evolutionism to the point that truth must be hidden and lies must be fabricated, and creation believing professors must be fired if they do not keep their mouths shut. All this in order to keep Darwinian evolutionism alive and kicking.

Dawkins is a product of his indoctrination by an "education system", his thoughts are not original, they were given to him throughout his education. His role models taught him to reject the idea of a God. School teachers and professors are often very skilled at making students feel dumb for not embracing their religion. Notice Dawkins will even go as far as to quote John Lennon lyrics from the *Imagine* song. *Imagine no God* ... When Stalin, Tung and Hitler imagined no God, the whole world got a real good glimpse of hell. Now that I have imagined no God and seen hell, would you be so kind as to imagine hell? It should be easier to do now that we have seen the results of imagining no God. We know that rock stars can be quite influential over young minds, making it seem like the cool thing to do to reject the idea of a God or to praise Satan. It's clear to see Dawkins is a person who gravitated toward the religion that his favorite role models embraced. Is that really any different than a child raised as a Mormon, whose role models are Mormon, growing up to be a Mormon? Or a child raised as a Muslim, whose favorite role models are Muslim, growing up to be a Muslim? It's really very common, and statistically probable. Dawkins choice of religion is not due to any deep thinking or musing on his part, as he would have his readers believe. Dawkins is simply embracing the religion of the role models that he most admired in life, and that is nothing new. Dawkins is not being lead by science, he is clearly being lead by blind faith. I would like to drive home some key points and reiterate a few points that I have already made...

- **Dawkins is a very religious person who places great faith in unscientific notions of the origins the of universe and the origins of life.**

-**Evolutionism (being preached at the taxpayer's expense) is a religion requiring constant and repetitious indoctrination techniques starting in preschool to get young minds to believe such fantastic, unscientific ideas.**

-**Public schools and universities (funded by tax dollars) are the religious seminaries for the students of and potential priests of evolutionism.**

-**Teachers and professors (paid by tax dollars) are actually the priests whose mission is to pedal their faith in the unscientific, fantastic religion of evolutionism.**

-**Textbooks (paid for by tax dollars) containing bogus information about a big bang, the age of the earth, geologic columns, and radiometric dating are the scriptures for the religion.**

-**Museums of Natural History (funded by tax dollars) are the temples of worship for the devotees of Darwinian evolutionism.**

Evolutionism is simply not lacking any of the components needed to fairly define it as a religion. Here we have great faith in things unseen and improvable. We have priests indoctrinating children at every learning level with zero tolerance for any other opinion or theory. Evolutionism has its great prophets declaring their unproven and improvable insights. Evolutionism has the exaltation of man by means of human sacrifice. Evolutionism has its seminaries and temples. Evolutionism has all the ingredients needed to fairly define it as a modern religion. However, there is one glaring difference between evolutionism and all of the other religions, evolutionism is funded by tax dollars. This religion is labeled "science" and is, in fact, intermingled with real science, we understand that, but that does not make evolutionism science.

The evolutionism religion is masked as science for two obvious reasons, one, because science is funded by tax payers, and two, so that it can be pedaled as fact to society's young, naive minds. Any rational person studying science would never conclude, based on observation, that evolution is the cause of energy, time, space, matter or life. Almost all people professing faith in evolutionism were repetitiously taught these lies over and over again since they were very young, this has been the key to the success of this state funded religion. Without the support of tax dollars, indoctrinating young minds from preschool, virtually nobody would be would be duped into swallowing this far out, fictitious, improvable, idiotic religion of evolutionism.

The Hidden Agenda

Could there be a father of all of these lies that lead one to believe in evolutionism and eventually human sacrifice? I believe that there is a father of this movement of lies and murder, and I believe he has a name. Could a religion as ridiculous as evolutionism really be driven by science? No, it's clear that this religion is spiritually driven. The defenders of this faith not only fanatically insist on the youth accepting their lies and rejecting creation, but they also viciously oppress any voice that would shed some light upon the truth. What spiritual forces could be behind this all out war against truth and liberty? Perhaps a review of the clearly stated policies of the Satanist's General Council of the 1700's would help us to better understand what spiritual forces are driving this aggressive and hostile religion's propaganda campaign. The General Council's policies for the coming age were as follows...

Satanism's General Council of the 1700's policy # 1
To deceive people about the existence of Satan and his angles, so they would not believe that they exist.

Satanism's General Council of the 1700's policy # 2
To have total control over the minds of people through hypnotism.

Satanism's General Council of the 1700's policy # 3
To destroy the Bible without burning it through the theory of evolution.

It is no mystery to me why the decades that followed these Satanic mandates would give birth to popular books like Charles Lyell's *Principles of Geology*, and Charles Darwin's book *The Origin of Species by Means of Natural Selection or*

the Preservation of Favored Races in the Struggle for Life.
These books would be passed off on a gullible society as science through lies and deception. This deception would ultimately give birth to the spiritually driven religion of modern evolutionism. So am I telling you that Satan is the God of evolutionism? That is exactly what I am telling you. Please read the polices of Satanism's General Council of the 1700's again, and then consider what has happened in the two consecutive centuries.

Huge portions of our society are now convinced that aliens from other planets exist, while they believe demons do not exist, unaware that contact with ET is really contact with demonic forces. We know that the Illuminati has ultimate influence in the US government, so that means that the Illuminati controls the CIA. Did you know that George H. Bush was once the director of the CIA? Did you know that he was also a member of the Skull and Bones secret society? Now you do. The CIA has spent billions on their ET propaganda campaign. The hardcore Satanists at the very top have gone to great lengths to sell this deception. Why? This is going to be the big global threat that will unite the nations for the NWO's Satanic global governing system.

...Woe to the inhabitants of the earth and the sea! For the devil has come down to you, having great wrath, because he knows that his time is short.
Revelation 12:12 NKJV

Our government has staged fake flying saucer crashes and fabricated alien corpse hoaxes. They have even duped many of their own agents into believing that ET is real. They have abducted, drugged and brainwashed people to give them memories of close encounters of the worst kind. Places like Area 51 are cloaked in secrecy because of the Satanic activity that goes on there, not because they are hiding ET from the public. Mutilated cattle that have all of their blood and organs removed with unprecedented, precision surgical accuracy is not the result of a curious ET, but the result of Satanic, supernatural, sacrificial rituals.

I want to reiterate, the Illuminati owns the media. They have leaked all the evidence we need to believe in aliens, except of course, the alien bodies for an autopsy by independent laboratories. They can use shows like *The X- Files* or movies like *Avatar* to give the public their needed visuals. This is another one of the Illuminati's massive population dupings.

There has been a plan in effect since at least 1917 to create an artificial Extraterrestrial threat to planet Earth, so as to bring about a one-world, Luciferian, totalitarian socialist government. This Extraterrestrial propaganda has been promoted through movies, through books, in the newspapers; so as to create the idea in the public mind that this phenomenon related to Extraterrestrials is real and that the threat is real. -William Cooper, former Navel Intelligence Officer, former Freemason and author of the best selling underground book of all times, the book is entitled *Behold a Pale Horse*.

In his book Cooper explains in great detail his knowledge of Illuminati controlled CIA conspiracies. Cooper exposes the UFO phenomenon for what it is, a Satanic propaganda campaign. Surprise, Cooper was shot and killed in a shoot out with the police, under very mysterious and suspicious circumstances at his home in Eagar, Arizona on November 6, 2001. The media called him a *"militia man"*. Cooper had no criminal record, nor did he have a cashe of weapons. Cooper was an honorably discharged, disabled veteran of the Vietnam war, who also served in Military Intelligence. Cooper's only crime was exposing the Illuminati's Extraterrestrial propaganda campaign. The following verse is the verse that inspired the title of William Cooper's book.

So I looked, and behold, a pale horse. And the name of him who sat on it was Death, and Hades followed with him. And power was given to them over a fourth of the earth, to kill with the sword, with hunger, with death, and by the beasts of the earth.
Revelation 6:8 NKJV

The US government has super advanced technology; aircrafts that would blow your mind; they can leave our atmosphere, return and submerge into water. This will seem like something from another planet to most of the world. Our government has flying cities that are up to two miles in diameter. They have underground FEMA cities and underground train networks connecting these cities. Could this be where trillions of tax dollars are disappearing to?

Recall from chapter two's section on organic evolution; I mentioned the emergence of genetic engineering technology that will be able to genetically alter test tube humans, like it hasn't already happened. Do you think that these hardcore Satanists at the very top have not been aggressively seeking to produce genetically altered minions, if they haven't already? Oh no, they would never do that, it is just not ethical, they must have boundaries of ethics that would prohibit them from doing such things. If you believe that ethics would prohibit the Illuminati from producing genetically altered humans, then I certainly envy your naivete. This may well be the science employed to give the world ET creatures to frighten the masses into doing just about whatever the government will tell them to do, like perhaps vaccinations against alien diseases (a death sentence). Will genetically altered humans have a soul? I don't know, I kind of doubt it. Could an army of freakish clones be engineered to be obey orders with ruthless obedience? Yes, this is no longer science fiction. This is the world we live in. This is the kind of demonically inspired, cutting edge technology that is cloaked in secrecy by the CIA in places like area 51. Pretty freaky, huh? In the occult, this is called "black science".

For they are spirits of demons, performing signs, which go out to the kings of the earth and of the whole world, to gather them to the battle of that great day of God Almighty. Revelation 16:14 NKJV

Combine the aircraft technology and the genetically altered human technology, and the world is in for a very convincing and persuasive duping. This could get really freaky. I don't think it will happen tomorrow, first legislation to revoke Americans' right to bear firearms will be passed and enforced. The way things are going, that shouldn't be too long. Would Satanists really go to these extremes to implement their global governing system? Yes they have, and yes they will continue to do so.

I am not convinced that huge portions of our society are hypnotized yet, however, I am not unconvinced. I am very certain that huge portions of society are brainwashed by the media, believing whatever comes across their TV screen or computer monitor. Video games, kid's movies and the internet are bombarding society with Satanic symbolism continuously. Some of the most seemingly innocent cartoons for toddlers will start unleashing information about how fun magic is, and the joys of being a witch, complete with spell castings and demonic symbolisms. I could consider this high tech electronic media assault as a form of hypnosis, I suppose. No doubt drugs, both pharmaceutical and street drugs, are having a hypnotic effect on huge portions of our society. The Illuminati influences the music industry, they have the ability to create and own recording artists in every genre. Illuminati driven music is geared to have hypnotic and sub-liminal effects on the public mind. I do not really believe that the Satanic Illuminati has total hypnotic control of over the minds of the people yet, but trust me, they are working on it.

Without a doubt the theory of evolution has been used as a means to destroy the Bible without burning it. Nearly the entire world has been duped into believing that the earth is billions of years old, with absolutely no scientific evidence to support such an absurd notion. The Illuminati has infil-trated science and filled textbooks with this lie of billions of years so they can make the ridiculous idea of evolution seem possible. The success of this campaign has sent millions and millions of souls to spend eternity in hell.

Please recall life's four fundamental questions from Chapter four. Do you recall evolutionism's answers to these questions? Lets see how those answers stack up against Satanism's answers to those same questions.You will find the answers to be pretty much synonymous, revealing the fact that the two religions are really the same religion. Remember what those questions were? Origin, meaning, morality and destiny.

Origin: Where did I come from?
Man has always created his gods, rather than his gods creating him. -Anton LaVey, *The Satanic Bible, Book of Lucifer 1:1*

Meaning: What is the meaning to life?
Life is the great indulgence, Death the great abstinence, therefore make the most of life HERE AND NOW! -Anton LaVey, *The Satanic Bible, Book of Satan 4:1*

Morality: Who defines right and wrong?
Do what thou wilt shall be the whole of the law.-Aleister Crowley, 33rd degree Freemason (Father of modern Satanism)

Destiny: Where will I go when I die?
There is no heaven of glory bright, and no hell where sinners roast. Here and now is our day of torment! Here and now is our day of joy! Here and now is our opportunity! Choose ye this day, this hour, for no redeemer liveth!
-Anton LaVey, *The Satanic Bible, Book of Satan 4:2*

What is the difference between the two religions? There is no difference! The answers to these fundamental questions are the same in both religions. The fact that human sacrifice is a necessary ritual in both religions makes the two religions identical. You see if they taught Satanism to our children, with zero tolerance for any other religion, then the public would fully rebel against it. So what is a cunning Lucifer to do? Call it evolution, weave it into the science textbooks and watch the carnage unfurl. Evolutionism is simply synonymous with Satanism. The only difference between an evolutionist and a Satanist is that the Satanist fully knows who is pulling their strings, while the evolutionist enjoys half hearted denial. Science vs. religion? Well, I guess it could be called science vs. religion; true creation science vs. the religion of Satanism. This is truth vs. Satanism, nothing less. Am I being dramatic? No, I am being factual. There is no need to mask the facts any longer. Evolutionism is built on the exact same pack of lies that Satanism is built on, making the two religions one. Sorry, I do not make the rules. I expose the facts.

Let's try to tie all of this together. Our nation is in reality being governed by the Satanic Illuminati, from behind the scenes. The US government was born out of the Illuminati's Freemasons, who were working toward building a new Atlantis, with the mission of orchestrating a Satanic global governing system. This Illuminati influenced government controls the youth's textbook content. Public education is a big part of this scheme. In accordance with Satanism's general council policy, evolutionism has been forced on society to destroy the Bible. The global Illuminati has enjoyed great success in this endeavor, especially in Europe and Asia. Their goal for a New World Order supersedes any loyalty to nations, governments or political parties. This achievement was the key to opening doors to more schemes by the Satanically driven Illuminati. We now have more people believing in space aliens than believing that Satan and demons exist. This is another huge success. Who is going to engage in spiritual warfare against enemy forces that they do not even believe exist? Oh, and now Satan can enjoy the sweet offerings of human sacrifices. Our nation now offers up 4,500 human sacrifices a day to the god of Satanism / evolutionism. What a success.

Guess what, this is just the tip of the ice berg. Recall the Illuminati's new Ten Commandments for the coming New World Order. There are big plans for a one world government, with a one world religion, which will be worshiping the anti-Christ (the devil incarnate), massive depopulation schemes and totalitarian, iron fisted, martial law... Coming soon to a theatre near you. Lucifer and his angels have been working for millennia to bring this plot into fruition, and according to the Bible they are going to achieve their goal for a short time. Given the numerous biblical clues and prophecies being fulfilled, I believe that we are very close to that time (within decades at the most). It is time to choose sides. If you get nothing else out of this book, please get this, evolutionism is not science, evolutionism is Satanism. The hidden agenda is entirely Satan's scheme to be empowered as the king of the entire world through a global governing system, and drag as many souls into hell as he possibly can before he is crushed by the Creator.

Human Sacrifices:

The clear teaching of the New Testament declares the need for one sacrifice to elevate man to the level of immortality, this was accomplished some 2,000 years ago on a wooden cross. The blood of Christ is the only bloodshed required for sinful man's redemption and immortality. Atheism, on the other hand, has a very sinister, murderous plot for man's exaltation. You see, the god of evolutionism / Satanism has an insatiable appetite for human life.

Atheism's religious leaders, the likes of Stalin, Tung and Hitler, have sacrificed enough human victims to fill every single sports stadium and concert arena in the world with dead bodies. Atheism's genocidal extermination machines roll on, as they continue to grind up, incinerate and mutilate millions and millions of humans. This nonstop mass murder by the multimillions started after the teachings of Charles Darwin became popular, which gave rise to the modern religion of evolutionism, in where death is fundamental to the plot. Death is a necessary ritual in the religion, often resulting in assembly line style, dead human body factories. How many human sacrifices will be enough to appease the god of evolutionism? Will evolutionism's thirst for blood ever be quenched?

Evolutionism has popularized and normalized the sacrifice of unborn and newborn children. Modern "science" wants to pretend that abortion is not really committing homicide. When a living human intentionally stops the beating heart of another living human that has posed no threat to anyone and is struggling for their little life, this is defined as homicide. No amount of fifty cent words or college degrees changes this fact. How does being small and unable to speak yet cancel your human rights?

There is a popular technique nowadays for aborting baby humans, which a lot of the public is not even aware of, it is called labor induced abortion. Late term pregnancies are terminated by giving the mother a labor inducing drug (oxytosin), the baby is born, often alive, then placed into medical waste trash bins while he or she is still breathing. The little child's receiving blanket is a red plastic bio-hazardous waste bag. After some time the newborn child will eventually die in the trash heap. This actually goes on in the good old USA. Barack Obama has actually voted for legislation to let children die that are alive and well outside of their mother's womb. This is called infanticide. Sadly, 93% of women who get an abortion will admit that they have lived to regret it, more than half of them will seek some form of psychological treatment to help them cope with life thereafter.

Another brutal sacrificial tactic is called partial birth abortion, that's when the child is cut into pieces and killed as he or she is being birthed. Little American babies will be sentenced to death, either before or shortly after being born. This is the amoral consequence of Darwinian evolutionism. How can anyone justify this insanity? Over 4,500 little US citizens will meet this fate today. Where is the outrage? Well over a billion little children have met this fate worldwide. That is why it is so important that we carefully examine the legislation records of any political candidate that we may consider voting for.

Visit **unplannedthebook.com** for some interesting information about how brave little unborn children with a beating heart, will fight with great determination against the the human butcher, just weeks after conception. Former planned parenthood director, Abby Johnson, tells her story of the horrors of the abortion clinic. Abby exposes the lies that are told to parents to comfort them as they are coerced into allowing their child to be killed.

If you have made the mistake of having had your child aborted and you are one of the 93% who admits to regretting it, then you may be carrying a certain amount of guilt. Understand that the only thing you could possibly do to try to right this wrong, is to confess it to God. You are already repenting, why not just seek forgiveness from the One who is now taking care of that child in heaven? He will be quick to forgive you. I want to believe that you read the prayer from chapter five with sincerity, now it's time to give this burden, this heartache, this regret to the Lord. He is just to forgive, and he is taking divine care of your child. He intends to reunite you with your child in paradise, and if you trust Him to do that, He will.

Now that we, as a society, are so comfortable terminating innocent children, the euthanasia agenda to rid our population of the sick, elderly and non productive members of society should be fully implemented with relative ease. This plan is well underway in the US, with no intentions of going away. Is there enough moral opposition to stop it? I hope so, because I may grow old, and my children may grow old.

When will atheists ever be satisfied? With this warp in human thinking, it should not be long before Hitler style extermination plans are implemented for the massive population reduction schemes. If you ever get bored, Google or Youtube **"FEMA coffins"** or **"FEMA concentration camps"** or *"chem trails,"* it will blow your mind, I promise. Since the ultimate New World Order plan is to reduce the human population to less than one half of one billion, that means that at least several billion people will need to be deposed of. Don't buy into this overpopulation propaganda, there is enough room in just the state of Texas alone, for every person on earth to have a big home in a huge yard. There is no shortage of food either. In the western world there is enough food thrown in the trash every day to feed the third world. The people that are starving in this world are not starving because of lack of food, but because of empowered mad men oppressing the less desirables, in their effort to rid the world of the "inferior species".

Did you know that today 25,000 humans will drop dead from hunger on this planet? This is the result of evolutionism / Satanism. There is plenty of room and plenty of food on this planet. Overpopulation is being propagated in an effort to justify a massive depopulation campaign. Since the reports of land and food shortages have proven to be bogus, perhaps "science" will trump up a new global emergency, something that sounds a little more sciencey; like "global warming" maybe. That would give the gods of this planet a new and improved excuse to offer massive human sacrifices to the god of evolutionism, and usher in their New World Order.

Am I am crazy enough to believe that history could repeat itself? Yes, I not only believe it could happen again, but I believe it will happen again.

Be warned about vaccines, I ask you to please visit the website **childhoodshots.com** for some eye opening information about vaccines before you have yourself or your child vaccinated. Mary Tocco's DVD, *Are Vaccines Safe?*, really opened my eyes to the ugly truth regarding vaccines. Mary did not go as far as to say that vaccines are a depopulation conspiracy, but I definitely see a connection. When you consider the huge spikes in autism (rendering reproduction unlikely) and SIDS after the vaccine requirements were enforced, you just have to give pause and entertain the possibility of evil men implementing evil plans, especially when you consider that these spikes in deadly diseases are even higher in the poorer areas. I am now forced to realistically consider that HIV was first introduced to the continent of Africa through vaccines in an effort to depopulate... It makes perfect Darwinian sense.

As a US citizen you still have the right to refuse a vaccine for yourself or your children (at least for the moment), but you will be given the impression that you absolutely must allow them to vaccinate your kids. Doctors will try many fear and intimidation techniques to get you to comply with the vaccine regiment, but you do have the right to refuse it. As a result of refusing vaccines, you will be put on the record as someone who has refused to comply, and the information will be put into a data base. Just try refusing a vaccine, wow, you will get lectured, ridiculed and belittled. This is bizarre because the doctor cannot even tell you what is in the vaccine. We have the right to know what's in our cookies and chewing gum, but the ingredients for vaccines remain a mystery. That's funny, but not ha ha funny.

Could the recent H1N1 "swine flu epidemic" that scared an entire population into demanding vaccines have been a test run to measure the compliance of the population in a "federal emergency", while generating enormous revenue? A dress rehearsal of sorts? A way to see if they could get an entire population to stand in line and demand their death sentence? I think it very well could have been. The pharmaceutical companies, which have a super powerful lobby in Washington, also made billions off of this H1N1 "epidemic". Governing agencies also gathered a huge amount of information at the same time.

Look on online for **"Bill Gates, vaccines to depopulate"**; he seems pretty forthright about using vaccines to depopulate. There is a whole committee of billionaires that seem to be self appointed saviors of the world, and they seem to believe that the only way to save mother earth is to rid the planet of the cancerous, human population. Since the food and land shortage excuse to depopulate is proven bogus under scrutiny, blood thirsty power brokers are now propagating the lie of global warming as their excuse to sacrifice huge portions of the world's population to Satan. Please see Hal Lindsey's report on the committee of death, its online, it is entitled **"Secret Billionaires Club - Bill Gate's Plan for Depopulation - Hal Lindsey "**. Hal is a lot more competent to explain what is going on than I am, and he does a great job of shining a light on some of the famous key players and their evil agenda.

The Bilderberg group sure seems to be part of the world domination plot. There is evidence that they are conspiring toward a New World Order that has plans for a massive depopulation campaign. The Bilderberg Group is a group of some 120 super rich power brokers, the Illuminati big shots. The Illuminati has it's tentacles in everything; science, entertainment, media, health care, pharmaceuticals, illegal drugs, sex trade, big oil, weapons of war, food distribution, banking, energy, automobiles, aircrafts, ships, real estate, computers, all of the highest technologies, all of the commodities; EVERYTHING! The Illuminati is profiting from just about everything. The Bilderberg group seems to have big plans for ushering in this NWO.

Be sure to see Governor Jesse Ventura's documentary, Youtube **Bilderberg Group: The Exclusive documentary**. Ventura's investigation blows their scheme wide open. The Illuminati is the hierarchy of all of these secret, satanic, blood oath societies. I have done extensive online research investigating the Illuminati, Freemasonry, Bohemian Club, Bilderberg Group, NWO, FEMA concentration camps, FEMA coffins and vaccines. I was hoping to tie it all together for the reader as an added bonus, but I will not need to do that because Ventura's documentary on this conspiracy really does shed more light on the subject than this book could. Ventura's investigation includes interviews with secret society insiders, reporters that have been following the Illuminati for decades, and medical doctors that have full knowledge of their depopulation intentions. Darwinian atheism's "science" agenda is really just smoke and mirrors for an ancient, satanic Illuminati plot that will be unfurled on humanity.

The devil, who deceived them, was cast into a lake of fire and brimstone where the beast and the false prophets are. And they will be tormented day and night forever and ever.
Revelation 20:10 NKJV

Don't let all this doom and gloom freak you out. If you are trusting in Christ, you have nothing to fear. Do not believe that your peace and safety will come from any worldly government or global governing system. The promises of a unified world living in harmony, under a flag of peace, may very well sound appealing to the masses, but those who trust the words of the Bible, know full well that a global governing system will only bring about the satanic, totalitarian, New World Order.

For you yourselves know perfectly that the day of the Lord so comes as a thief in the night. For when they say, "Peace and Safety!" then sudden destruction comes upon them, as labor pains upon a pregnant woman. And they shall not escape. But you brethren, are not in darkness, so that this Day should not overtake you as a thief. I Thessalonians 5: 2-4

Let's suppose that we believers find ourselves living in a satanic, tyrannical NWO, with Satan himself at the helm. Let's consider the possibility that we may not get raptured off of this planet before the mustard hits the fan. Personally, I cannot find overwhelming evidence that the believers, alive on earth, will be raptured out of this time of great tribulation. I hope that believers are spared this event, but it remains a mystery to me. Let's not be caught off guard if we wind up alive on planet earth for this great tribulation. We would live as fugitives, trying to stay below the radar of the NWO, unable to buy and sell. Perhaps on a most wanted list, perhaps not. This tribulation period will last for seven years. Staying true to the Living God during this period would require great faith, endurance and strength. No matter what anyone does to me, I will never bow to the antichrist, I will never submit to his authority, even if they burn me at the stake. What's the worst that anyone can do to us? Kill us? So what! We are going to spend eternity with Christ. Death has absolutely no sting.

And fear not them which kill the body, but are not able to kill the soul: but rather fear him which is able to destroy both soul and body in hell.
Matthew 10:28 KJV

O death, where is thy sting? O grave, where is thy victory?
I Corinthians 15:55 KJV

Chapter Nine

Government Mandated Religion

Communistic Visions of Utopia

"How could any decent person think it's right to label four-year-old children with the cosmic and theological opinions of their parents?"
Richard Dawkins, *The God Delusion*

Communism, is that your final answer? Why stop at a state funded religion, lets shoot for a government mandated totalitarian, indoctrination system. Dawkins don't want a child's cosmic and theological views to reflect that of the parents, no ladies and gentlemen, Dawkins wants the children's views to reflect Dawkins' cosmic and religious views. Classic case of a cult style mind set, squirming at the thought of anyone having a world view that opposes, or in some cases disproves his chosen religion.

I will agree that there are some pretty wacky religions out there, but it is not for us to decide what religious ideals a parent chooses to believe in or instill in their children. To revoke a parent's right to think freely is absurd, and that smells an awful lot like communism to me. I have only seen communism lead to the brutal murder of innocent people that did not agree with the all seeing, all knowing, dictatorship government that knows what is best for the citizens to believe. Fortunately, we here in the United States do not live in this utopian world that Dawkins envisions (at least for the moment), with all children being taught that God does not exist from the time they are four years old. Adolph Hitler, Joseph Stalin and Mao Tse-Tung certainly did share Dawkins' utopian dreams for the New World Order, and where would mankind be without their contributions to humanity?

Listen up Richard, it is your right to present your case for what you believe and why you believe it, but leave other people's children alone. Trying to steal the minds of our four year old children really makes you look pretty evil, especially now that we all know that evolutionism is really a mask for Satanism. I would never argue that dangerous fanaticism isn't wrong, but if one is not harming others in the practice of their religion, then they ought to be free to raise their kids in whatever religion they choose. The most harmful and dangerous of all these crack pot religions is unarguably the religion of evolutionism.

Dawkins of all people should be thrilled that the public schools with their secular, atheistic agenda have the minds of the children starting in kindergarten, for six hours a day, five days a week in which to indoctrinate the children with improvable, evolutionary fairytales, fabricated "evidence" and flat out lies. It starts with the Dr. Seuss books before kindergarten... *"Millions of years ago dinosaurs..."*. Preschoolers minds are rattled by the *Dinosaur Train,* this is a cute little cartoon series that comes on PBS daily. The show is filled with cute little dinosaurs that grab the attention of preschoolers. The show is aggressive evolutionism propaganda that attacks the mind of preschoolers without relent, telling toddlers lies like dinosaurs laid bird eggs, while stressing a fictitious geologic column and millions of years in every single episode. You see ladies and gentlemen, it's ok to teach the children lies, just as long as those lies support Dawkins' cosmic and theological views. Dawkins' was not alive millions of years ago, so he cannot know with any certainty that there was even an earth, much less dinosaurs millions of years ago. Let's not forget Dawkins' sound evidence... *"The layer of strata tells us the age of the fossils"* while *"The fossils tell us the age of the layer of strata"*. Dawkins that is not scientific reasoning so quit pushing your religion on our kids.

Once you understand that evolutionism is really Satanism, it really kind of turns your stomach when you see these prophets of the religion aggressively attacking the minds of innocent children. To me, Dr. Scott from the *Dinosaur Train*, looks just plain evil as he does his best to charismatically persuade innocent little toddlers to believe in evolutionary origins, as he drags young minds into the course of Satanism 101. Give it a look and tell me that nothing demonic is going on.

So Dawkins' religion teaches the earth is billions of years old with no sound evidence to support such a claim. My religion teaches the earth is not billions of years old, and there is plenty of scientific evidence to support such a claim. So as Dawkins' cries out, teach the children based on "science", he wants everyone to ignore the overwhelming evidence that the sun, moon and planets offer for a young universe. He wants us to teach other people's children his fairytale fantasy of how things came to be. This is beyond absurd when you consider that Dawkins' himself, admittedly, is not even 100% sure that he is right. You see Richard, it is that very freedom to believe and teach what we see fit to our children, that has afforded you the liberty to put faith in your crack pot, far out religion that has zero scientific evidence to support it. Even Dawkins, a devout atheist, is not even 100% convinced he is right by his own admission... but he wants children taught as fact this religion of evolutionism that he is not even 100% sure about. That is funny, but not ha ha funny. In China, it is a crime to teach a child about any God until they reach the age of 18. Perhaps China should set the world standard on human rights and ethical treatment of children. How could any decent person deprive a child of a God in which they can take refuge when there is no one else in the world to turn to?

The boys who orchestrated the Columbine CO school massacre were self proclaimed devotees of evolutionism. They saw it fitting to commit their murderous acts on Hitler's birthday, as they shared his religious and world views. Let's suppose that those boys would have had a God to take refuge in, or a God to be accountable to. What if those boys would have had Jesus as their role model as opposed to Nazi, mad man Adolph Hitler?

In Tucson AZ, Jared Lee Loughner, an atheist, Marxist gunman went on a shooting rampage in an effort to kill his state's congress woman. Jared managed to shoot her in the head, kill a federal judge and kill and wound other innocent bystanders. That is a tragedy. What is ironic is that the media blamed the conservative right, when it was the liberal left's atheistic agenda that paved the way for Jared to be educated in a Darwinian education system. Jared needs God, but because of his education, Jared is convinced that he shares a common heritage with cockroaches, and that the fittest survive by killing off their competition. I wonder if Jared was humming the *imagine* tune as he attempted to put in a second clip of ammunition.

Cold, callus, calculated murder seems to be the eventual result of Satanic evolutionism. How could any decent person deprive a child of a God to hold them accountable for their behavior? How could any decent person deprive a child of the forgiving, unconditional love that God has to offer children who are simply not getting this love from anywhere else? What gives anyone the right to mandate that a child must be deprived of having peaceful faith in their Creator? Dawkins wants the school to instill the unchecked religion of Darwinian evolutionism on children with zero tolerance for parental influence on a child's thought process. I ask you, how could this line of reasoning be anything but demonic?

Defend the Children

Of course brainwashing children is wrong. Teaching children to hate others is wrong. It is a shame that in the name of a god people would actually take pride in persuading their own children to strap on bombs and go blow themselves up in a crowd of innocent people. Wicked men have done it all in the name of their god, brainwashing, fear tactics, rape, murder, torture, human sacrifice, it couldn't get more wicked. I certainly cannot deny the insanity that religion has inflicted upon humanity. The most insane and dangerous of all religions is provably the religion of evolutionism / Satanism. So in defense of children, we as a society must refrain from teaching children any type of religion in the public schools, but tragically children are taught the most dangerous of all the religions, the religion of evolutionism.

Children can get their religion at home; it is not the job of the state to marry education and religion, but that is exactly what they have done, and if Dawkins had his way, the whole world would be forced to ingest this state funded religion. Why don't we educate the children with reading, writings, science and math and allow the parents to share their views of God with their child. Hopefully the child would grow up, look at the facts and draw their own conclusions. What I was taught growing up, both in the schools and in the home are a far cry from my current world views and theological views. I just looked at the facts, the science and the data. It's like I had no choice but to believe what makes the most sense and disbelieve what is disprovable and nonsense. Does my view of eternity constitute faith? Sure, but it takes more faith to believe the evolution scheme than any other religion. I will still refer to my faith in God as just that, faith, but the over-whelming scientific evidence gives me no cause to reject the fact that there is a Creator, and no existing evidence could possibly persuade me to accept evolutionism.

It is sad that in the name of religion many children are abused, incited to intolerance or "racism" and brainwashed into such great fear that they will do anything that their personal "spokesmen for god" will tell them to do, including torturing fellow humans or homicidal bombings. I would never deny that this is sickening and awful. Kids who grow up in fearful submission to a spokesman for god, and believing that this spokesperson holds the keys to their eternal destiny, have a very difficult time learning to think for themselves. Sadly, they may never learn to think for themselves because spokesmen for god usually manipulate young minds in order to get children to conform to their expectations and traditions. Manipulation by fear, guilt, shame or condemnation is all too common and easy to instill on a child. I am not excusing the members of any religion, but we as a society cannot afford to let any government mandate their Satanic ideologies upon our children, the results have never been anything but hideous and bloody.

Wake Up Call

Please hear this wake up call, for the sake of the kids. Anyone that may be using intimidation or condemnation techniques to control a child's theological thought process. You are depriving that child of the ability to clearly think for his or herself. That will, without a doubt, make the child's life more difficult. I am not against time-outs or spankings for child behavior modification (not done in anger, but in love, with a detailed explanation of what infraction warranted the spanking). I am very much against using any mind manipulating methods to form a child's view of God to be such that when the child disappoints the spokesmen, they are somehow condemned and no longer hold their status as one of God's eternal children. If you are a religious person who is doing that, then you are doing a great disservice to that child, even if you call yourself a Christian. You certainly do not have that child's interests above your own selfish, control freakish interests. Let us never judge a child's eternal status. Never let yourself or your child make the mistake of believing that any person is an infallible spokesman for God. There are plenty of control freaks out there, who would just love to take God's job... I am sorry, but the position has already been filled.

I just cannot bag on religion, without bagging on the most dangerous one of them all. Evolutionists are as guilty as any of the other religions in their lust for the minds of children, not just their own children, but for my children and your children. Keep in mind the evolutionist has many more hours per week in which to work on a child's mind, so they can be very repetitious and persuasive. We all know that repetition is the mother of all skill, also know that repetition is the mother of all brainwashing tactics. Atheists are just as adamant about controlling the child's theological thought process as any of the other religions, of course this is accomplished through psychological persuasion and intimidation techniques in the institutions of learning. Let us never forget what happens when the evolutionary priests have risen to power in certain nations; the fear, intimidation and human disposal machines get turned on full blast.

I cannot stress this next point enough, so please hear this loud and clear, moms and dads, GET YOUR KIDS OUT OF PUBLIC SCHOOLS!!! Do whatever it takes but get them out, for the sake of your child's future, get them out. For the sake of humanity's future, get them out.

In all fairness, I would like to mention the fact that my first son, Christian, went to kindergarten in a public school in Sarasota. His kindergarten teacher, Mr. David Jones, was one of the finest and most effective teachers I have ever met. Mr. Jones had my child reading in a matter of weeks. My son actually wanted to go to school, even when he was sick, because he wanted to see his teacher / friend Mr. Jones. I fully understand that there are many well meaning, capable, effective, noble teachers in the public schools, but they do not control the textbook content. It is their job to present the textbook content, even when those textbooks contain lies and Darwinian propaganda. The risk is too great, you need to get your kids out of public schools. Please consider that you really cannot afford not to. Remember, garbage in, garbage out.

Most states have programs that will pay for a private school if you are moving the child out of public schools to protect them from the religion of evolutionism, and cannot afford a private school. Find a private school and ask them about the programs available, if they do not have solid answers about financial assistance, then try other private schools. If you persist you should be able to get some results. Don't tire and give up, this is way too important. This is your child.

Wouldn't it be horrible to live in a nation where you were forced to wear a beard or a burka, or to bow for hours every day facing Mecca? Wow, that would be horrible. I hate to even imagine it being imposed upon me or my family, it just seems so insane. However, a fascist, tyrannical theocracy is, by comparison, a pretty safe and peaceful place to live when you look at the sheer insanity unleashed on humanity by the prophets of evolutionism. No need for me to go on about all the work camps, death camps, and genocidal extermination machines. I would feel a lot safer in a fascist, theocratic nation than I would in a nation with an evolutionist dictator at the helm. I have never seen any studies done on this, but I hypothesize that children would much rather grow up in a land where they are forced to wear a burka, as opposed to a land where they, along with their families, are being herded into meat grinders by atheist mad men. I just have a hunch that my hypothesis is accurate. SO IN DEFENSE OF CHILDREN, let the government mandate NO religious view on our youth, especially the most brutal and violent religious view of them all, evolutionism / Satanism.

Chapter Ten

The Gap Delusion

Filling the Gap

Is God really just a much needed gap in the human brain? An imaginary friend, father, brother, confessor or confidant that humans so desperately want to believe is real? Is that all that God is? That's what Dawkins claims he believes. I have no problem believing that some brains may have gaps in them, and the more you listen to a Darwinian evolutionist ramble; the easier it is to believe that perhaps some brains have some serious gaps in them. Dawkins contends that we should fill our God need gaps with something other than God, like science, art, human friendship or humanism... Alright, maybe Dawkins has filled a gap in his brain with something that is not God, understood.

I cannot understand why a rational person would surrender an inherent need to know their Creator for products of His creation. One will never know science if one does not know the Creator, one can pretend, and use lots of big 50 cent words, they can even acquire a whole string of letters to follow their name, but that does not explain away all that is in the creation that simply declares the reality of a Creator. Refusing to believe in a Creator is not at all based on science, it is simply a classic case of stubborn denial.

We know that art is a product of the imagination; so how could one begin to fathom true artistry if they have never known the original Designer? They may think that they know art, and they may be part of a social group that declares them artsy, but I tell you for sure, without God there is no art. I look at the sun setting over the sea, or at a full rainbow, or at a sky filled with stars and think, WOW, what awesome artistry our Creator demonstrates. An evolutionist looks and then reasons, WOW, look what a speck vomited up. To try to fill the void that is your need for God with a substitute like art, is really to deprive one's self of ever realizing true artistry.

Replace God with human friendship? I guess Dawkins forgot that one of the fundamentals of Darwinian atheism is the survival of the fittest, you know, might is right, squash the weaker species, it's your evolutionary birth right. This way of thinking doesn't leave a whole lot of room for friends. More than a billion humans have been slain under the brutal hammer of Darwinian atheism, now that just don't seem too friendly. Forcing God out of the minds of a society does not result in warm and friendly people. On the contrary, this results in cold, paranoid citizens under martial law.

Perhaps we should fill our God need gap with humanism. Okay, the truth is really starting to ooze now. More superior, more god like super humans could emerge if we would just eliminate those not contributing to the highly evolved gene pool, then the gene pool could evolve mankind into god status eventually. We should just fill our god need gap with anything, just not a belief in God, because that would hinder our ability to evolve into homo sapiens sapiens sapiens, thus becoming the god of our own world (that is humanism in a nutshell).

Humans could become God? Now where have I heard that lie before? Ah yes, that was the very first deception that Satan ever pulled on mankind, the oldest trick in the book. I have no hunger for any fruit that holds promises of enlightening me to the realization that I am God. There is no recipe for becoming God. It is only by the grace of God that there is a plan for our redemption. We are privileged to worship our Creator and stand in awe when considering all of the great things that He has created.

I would strongly advise anyone who has considered taking Dawkins' advice to busy your mind with art, science, friendships or humanism in an effort to help them ignore God, to ask yourself these few questions; Is trying to push God out of my mind for conscience free living here on earth worth trading my soul for? Is the approval of a community of professor brainiacs really worth an eternity estranged from God? Does denying the existence of God really make me seem more intellectual or more open minded? I hope your answers to these questions are no, no and no. There is no scientific reason to deny a Creator, likewise, there is no scientific reason to accept evolutionism.

Examining Gaps

Let's talk about some real gaps, not products of an evolutionary psychology theory or the imagination, but of true science. Let's examine some gaps that simply refuse to conform to evolutionism.

The gap between the moon and the earth for example... We are losing the moon at a rate of at least a couple of centimeters per years. So after 4.6 billion years, why is the moon still here? It should have left it's orbit around earth a billion years ago. Perhaps, two billion years ago the moon was orbiting the earth where the birds fly, pulling the tide over every inch of land on a daily basis. It just don't add up, the earth and moon simply could not possibly have had a 4.6 billion year relationship. I find it interesting that for the first moon voyage, the landing gear on the space craft was fitted with giant snow shoes so that the space craft would not sink deep down into billions of years of accumulated moon dust. For some reason the moon only had 6,000 years worth of moon dust on it. Scientists forgot to consider that perhaps aliens were visiting the moon every 6,000 years and vacuuming up the moon dust. Those aliens are probably compulsive, clean freaks.

Consider the gap between the sun and the planets like Mercury, Venus, and Earth. Let us consider the fact that the sun is burning up 600 million cubic tons of hydrogen per second. The sun would have been so big 4.6 billion years ago that Mercury and Venus would have been incinerated. How did the earth's atmosphere and water stay intact? The earth could not have sustained life with a sun so big and so close. Drip a drop of water onto a red hot skillet to get a good visual of the relationship between the earth and the sun 4.6 billion years ago. The fact that Mercury, Venus and Earth are even here is clear evidence that the sun-earth relationship cannot possibly fit into the scheme of evolutionism.

Let's examine the gap between the planet Saturn and the rings around it. The rings around Saturn are disappearing like smoke rings, simply dissipating... after 100 thousand years these rings should have been long gone, yet they remain. This is evidence that a creation took place recently... Once you take away billions of years, the whole idea of a rock evolving into plants and people becomes obviously ridiculous.

What about the earth's temperature? We all know that deep in the earth is magma (hot stuff). How long can a planet stay hot anyway? Millions of years? Not likely. Billions of years? No way! When you take a baked potato out of the oven and place it on a plate and leave it there, the next day you will discover that the potato is cold, it won't even melt butter. So if this earth is 4.6 billion years old... Why is it not cold yet? Why? The earth simply cannot be billions of years old, or it would have cooled off by now. Perhaps highly evolved space aliens are visiting planet earth every 30 thousand years to pump hot lava into the center of the earth. Those aliens sure are sneaky.

This planet is spinning fast. The earth is slowing down at such a rate that it loses at least a half second per year. This gradual decline in speed requires men to adjust the atomic clock on a regular basis to compensate for the slowing of the earth's rotation, it's called a leap second. So that means that 4.6 billion years ago the earth was spinning billions of seconds faster. So how did this "pre biotic soup" (that was peculating the first organism, the mother of every plant and animal) stay put? How could this soup (that hatched life) that was created by millions of years of rain on a rock (a rock that is still hot I might add) manage to stay glued to an earth spinning at that rate of speed? The earth is simply not billions of years old or it would have stopped spinning by now. Why let scientific facts get in the way of such a great religion?

This world we live on is one big magnet, that's why planet earth has a north pole and south pole. For 50 years, the strength of this magnetic field has been recorded by scientists. At the rate we are losing the strength of this magnetic field, this planet should be a rock without a magnetic field in just a few thousand years. If our magnetic field's strength is declining at such a rate, that tells a scientist that it used to be stronger. 20,000 years ago the earth's magnetic field would have been so great that planet earth could not have sustained life, just 20,000 little years ago. The evolutionist will scramble for improvable lies about reversals and magnetic resuscitations but that is pure fantasy. Science tells us that if there had been an earth 20,000 years ago, it could not have sustained life. Evolutionism, which is not science, contends we live on a magnetic yo-yo that would require alien wizards to come along and resuscitate this magnet that we live on every 10- 15 thousand years. Those aliens sure are sneaky.

Evolutionism / Satanism has not laid the foundations of their religion on mount improbable, they have actually laid the foundations of their religion on mount impossible. If Dawkins' book *The God Delusion* is the best case that the modern atheism religious movement can make for their blind faith in evolutionism, then we can conclude that the devotees of evolutionism have traded rational thinking for religious fantasy. This fantasy is truly more fantastic than any of the other religions. I will not go out of my way to offend Mr. Dawkins, but nor shall I don kid gloves when addressing the sheer absurdities that one must fabricate and ingest to place their faith in this evil, satanic religion that is masked as science.

Thank You

I want to thank my Lord and Savior Yeshua / Jesus for enabling me to author this book. Through all of my life's experiences that seemed to have no rhyme or reason, I know that You will make sense of it. Through all of my sins and mistakes, I know that You have forgiven me and that You can make it work out so that something good will become of it. Through all the hatred, betrayal and injustice that this world has leveled at me, I can endure. Thanks to You, I can forgive. Thank You Lord for my salvation, thank You Lord for creating me, thank You for this joyful life, thank You for Your awesome creation.

I want to thank my family. My beautiful wife Anna, thanks for putting up with the glow of the monitor when you were in bed trying to sleep, as I was pecking out this book. Thank you most of all for the three beautiful children, you are the best mom in the world, and the kids and I know it. Thank you Anna for loving me even when I have been less than loveable. Thank you my children; Christian, Christianna and Christopher for being in my life. Such little children are such great big, huge, enormous blessings, just watching you sleep blesses me to indescribable joy. My treasures are in heaven, true, but you little gifts from God are truly priceless treasures in this life. I will never forget the fact you are God's children, His creation, and He has blessed me with the privilege of raising you.

Thanks mom and dad, for raising me in a loving environment, and for trying your best to make me into a healthy, honest, hard working man. If I had it to do over again, I would not have been so disobedient, dishonest and disrespectful. I would not have survived to make it to the fulfilled life that I am now enjoying, if you would not have loved me so much. Thank you for your prayers and thank you for your forgiveness.

Thank you Kent Hovind, for opening up so much truth about science, creation and evolutionism. Thank you for caring about people that you don't know. Thank you for your great effort to reach the lost and confused victims of Darwinian evolutionism. Thank you for teaching the truth, with love being the only motive. God's peace be with you brother Kent. God bless you.

Thank you Victor Mitchell, for telling me that I had it in me to write this book, and then challenging me to do so. You have been my friend since we were in junior high. You have fought the same kind of demons that I have fought, and through Christ we have triumphed. God bless you.

Thank you Jonathan Bernis, for hounding me to stay on the right path, even when I resented you for it, when it just seemed easier to quit trying to fight the good fight. Thank you for your ministry that provides healthcare, love and truth to the most destitute people on this sin ravaged planet. Thank you for being the real deal in a world of shady deals. Shalom Jonathan. God bless you.

Thank you Chip Ingram, Ravi Zacharias, Chuck Swindol, Erwin Lutzer and David Jeremiah. You men have had a great impact on my life. I have heard hundreds of your messages via Moody radio, and I have been blessed and strengthened by every single one of them. You should know that your practical and biblical instructions are giving nourishment to so many spiritually hungry listeners. Keep up the good work brothers. May God bless everyone of you.

Thank you Richard Dawkins, for making such a weak case against creation, it was so easy to rebut. Thank you for the inspiration to write my first book. I want to thank you in advance for sincerely weighing the evidence and drawing a different conclusion. Please consider that God has not rejected you. I had a lot of fun reciprocating the abrasiveness toward your religion, so you may find this hard to believe, but I do love you man. One of my biological brothers, who is named Richard, died in 2004. I look forward to the day when I will call you brother Richard.

Perhaps you are you interested in buying copies of *The Dawkins Delusion Exposed* for loved ones who have been victims of the evolutionism propaganda campaign. Perhaps you are interested in buying additional copies for a college campus ministry or for a youth ministry. The cost of books is greatly discounted when purchased in quantity. Please be sure to visit the official website, **thedawkinsdelusionexposed.com** to place an order. This book may well serve as the ounce of prevention needed to avoid a ton of maintenance. This book may very well be the key to unlocking the shackles of evolutionism that are binding huge portions of our society.

CPSIA information can be obtained at www.ICGtesting.com
Printed in the USA
LVOW081340150212

268816LV00001B/32/P